HIDDEN NOTTINGHAMSHIRE

Days Out With a Difference

Tony Shaw

SIGMA
Leisure

Copyright © T. Shaw, 1998

All Rights Reserved. No part of this publication may be reproduced, stored in a retrieval system, or transmitted in any form or by any means – electronic, mechanical, photocopying, recording, or otherwise – without prior written permission from the publisher.

Published by Sigma Leisure – an imprint of
Sigma Press, 1 South Oak Lane, Wilmslow, Cheshire SK9 6AR, England.

British Library Cataloguing in Publication Data
A CIP record for this book is available from the British Library.

ISBN: 1-85058-624-1

Typesetting and Design by: Sigma Press, Wilmslow, Cheshire.

Cover Design: MFP Design & Print

Cover photographs: clockwise from top left – The Druid's Stone; Drakeholes; Titchfield Park; Gash bus, Elston (Tony Shaw)

Printed by: MFP Design & Print

Preface

The aim of this book is to acquaint the readers – either natives of the county or strangers to it – with a number of features in Nottinghamshire that are a little removed from inclusions in an ordinary county guide. Some of the subjects in the book may themselves be well known, a lot more will be less so, and a few others will be positively obscure. But all have one thing in common: the hidden element is their history. *Hidden Nottinghamshire* uncovers the mystery. Whether it is a pub, church, bridge, custom, canal, eccentric character, brewery, windmill, school or any one of a host of other things, the history of it is revealed. In the process, much of the history of the county also begins to take shape, although there is barely a mention of Robin Hood!

An in-depth account of all the one hundred features is clearly not within the scope of the book, but even those who know a lot about the county should find plenty to interest them. To name just a few items, you will discover: why the Anglo-Scotian Mills are so called; where Nottinghamshire's Gretna Green was; why Nan Scott locked herself away in a church for weeks; and how a theatre came to be built in a tiny village.

With one exception,* all the listed features can be seen today – the author has visited them – and clear directions are given to the sites. An Ordnance Survey street atlas of the county is nevertheless advisable, and for this reason grid references are marked. Almost all the places are plainly visible from the roadway or public footpath, although where this is not the case, the book states so.

In alphabetical order by geographical location, the book lists places by their more precise name – for example, names such as Radford and Sneinton are used, although strictly speaking they are inside

---

* This is Gedling Windmill, which had only a brief life, although Gedling House in the background of the picture is still very much in existence. My excuse for the topic's inclusion is that Zakariah Barrett, clearly one of the county's great eccentrics, deserves at least a few words. I am not aware of any other publication where his name has featured.

the city boundary, and the name Swingate is used even though it is within the parish of Kimberley.

My thanks go to: Bob and Wendy Beever of the Pauncefote Arms; George Dawson for his information on Saundby; Pete McCoy for explaining some aspects of bell-ringing and cricket; Roy Plumb for his assistance with Kimberley, Swingate and Watnall; Alan Smith and Sandra Scott for showing me round Littleborough toll-house; Maureen Rawson for the sketches; and, of course, the indefatigable Penny Atkinson, whose help, enthusiasm and forbearance have been indispensable.

1. Averham

The little theatre in the village

Grid Reference: 766544

Directions: Staythorpe is 3 miles west of Newark. Turn into Church Lane east of Staythorpe Road and park in a space opposite the lane leading to the rectory. The theatre is in the lane on the immediate left.

The sight of a theatre in the rural setting of the small village of Averham (pronounced "airum" locally) at first seems a bit out of place, like the Kinema in the Woods at Woodhall Spa, Lincolnshire. But the theatre has survived – with the exception of a few years' closure – since the beginning of the 20th century. It has an interesting history.

The founder of the Robin Hood Theatre was the Averham vicar, Revd Joseph Walker, a man who had travelled extensively and whose interests ranged from hunting to photography, but whose second big-

The Robin Hood Theatre

gest love next to the church was the theatre. He had cut his dramatic teeth at the Oxford Union Dramatic Society, where his ability as an actor was matched by his production skills and scenic artistry. Walker's Robin Hood Operatic Society began by staging productions in the village schoolhouse, putting on five performances of *Little Red Riding Hood*, an original fairy extravaganza, in December 1887. The entire cast consisted of members of the Walker family and the libretto was written by Walker.

But Walker was not content with this: he wanted a proper theatre designed specifically for the purpose. In 1912 he announced his intention to build a wooden theatre in the rectory gardens. Carpenter Robert Lee was his principal assistant and the 160-seater Robin Hood Opera House, as it was called then, was opened in 1913 in a village of 200 inhabitants. It cost £100 to build. The Rev. Walker, conscious of the necessity to attract mainly outside interest, was always careful to mention "full-moon week" in his advertisements – to entice people who might be discouraged by the bad lighting conditions on the country roads. The theatre succeeded: specialising in light opera, the Robin Hood drew the gentry and other country people to its box office. The Revd Walker continued with his theatre until his death in 1942, when G.P. Bennett carried on the work.

In the early 1950s, however, the theatre was forced to close because of alterations required by fire regulations. For some time the theatre was under threat of permanent closure due to lack of funds for the necessary work. But its fortunes were revived by the enthusiastic efforts of the rector, Bishop Mark Way, and financial assistance from Valerie Baker. The theatre was reopened in October 1961 for its first new production since the closure. Sir Donald Wolfit, who had played there as a schoolboy, was present at the occasion. The Robin Hood Theatre has continued ever since.

2. Babworth

A Queen stays at the inn

Grid Reference: 673798

Directions: Babworth is 2 miles west of Retford and Rushey Cottages are 1 mile south-west of Babworth village. The cottages are on the west side of the Mansfield Road just north of its junction with the Old London Road.

Now known as Rushey Cottages, of which there are three, this property was once Rushey Inn, the centre of a group of buildings suitable for a royal party to stay at. It is one of the many places in Nottinghamshire where highwayman Dick Turpin is said to have stayed, and a room in the pub was named after him. In 1503 Princess Marga-

The former Rushey Inn

ret Tudor, the daughter of Henry VII, spent the night here. Four years before her birth, Henry had brought an end to the War of the Roses by defeating Richard III at the Battle of Bosworth Field in 1485. James IV of Scotland had renewed the "auld alliance" with France and continued hostilities with England for a time, but now the King of England's daughter was on her way to marry him in Edinburgh. The event was intended to unite the two countries in peace and friendship.

Margaret's arrival at Babworth was a festive occasion: many people walked from Retford just to catch a glimpse of her, and there were minstrels and malmsey wine for the royal suite. Large numbers of people continued to follow the entourage as it made its way to Barnby Moor. The Archbishop of York's palace was at Scrooby (*q.v.*), and it was there that Margaret met Archbishop Savage and spent the next night. Travelling north, the princess passed up the Great North Road to Edinburgh.

The marriage was not to be a long one, however. When his brother-in-law Henry VIII declared war on France, James was under great pressure to attack the English. He did so, and was killed by the Earl of Surrey at the Battle of Flodden in 1513. Margaret became a widow at 24.

3. Barnby Moor

When stagecoaches ruled the roads

Grid Reference: 662845

Directions: Ye Olde Bell is on the Great North Road (A638), 2 miles north-west of Retford. It is just south of the junction with the A634.

Ye Olde Bell has stood for over three centuries, although for a short time as a private dwelling. It saw the great days of the stagecoaches and highwaymen before a different form of transport caused it to lose favour. As Scrooby declined in importance, Barnby Moor came into its own. Being on the busy Great North Road, it was ideally situated to capture through traffic.

In 1680 antiquarian and historian Ralph Thoresby of Leeds was returning home on horseback in a group. He and his friends had stayed the night in Newark and were now making their way to the Bell for the night. One of the party was drunk, however, and Thoresby had been delegated to take care of him. They lost their way and arrived at Tuxford, where Thoresby's intoxicated companion refused to move on. Thoresby left him at a hotel and journeyed on alone to Barnby Moor, arriving before the others. He visited the inn on at least two other oc·casions and found it very impressive.

By 1727 the Bell was becoming famous as a place to stay for the night. Arthur Young stayed there while gathering material for his Northern Tour and noted that in this area oxen, rather than the usual horses, were used for ploughing.

But it was the strong personality of George Clarke that made the Bell such a popular place between 1800 and 1842. He was always full of stories of interest and was a former sportsman and horse breeder. It was said that the inn was as well provided as a nobleman's castle, with stable room for 120 horses and 60 post boys. When "Captain

Ye Olde Bell – once a famous coaching house

Swing" (a kind of Luddite group) were setting fire to farm property nearby, Clarke found the culprits and turned them over to the police.

Although Clarke died a wealthy man, the next landlord was ruined by the Great Northern Railway: the age of the great coaching houses was giving way to technological advance. For 60 years the Bell was a private dwelling divided into two houses with part of it used as a chapel. It is only the arrival of private transport that has revived it.

4. Beeston

A new industry for Beeston

Grid Reference: 526372

Directions: Beeston is 4 miles south-west of Nottingham. The Anglo-Scotian Mills are near the corner of Wollaton Street and Albion Street.

The impressive and wonderfully symmetrical Anglo-Scotian Mills stand four storeys high with tall Victorian Gothic windows and a crenellated parapet. The entrance is said be modelled on nearby Thrumpton Hall.

Frank Wilkinson from Hucknall originally established his curtain lace business on this site. He had been a manufacturer of Shetland shawls, mantles and scarves when he took over the derelict Felkin factory. Beeston had previously traded in narrow lace, but this was the first time a curtain lace business had come to the town. He continued to use the name of his previous company: Anglo-Scotian Works. Wilkinson added buildings to the site until the whole business was centred in one area, from design and manufacture, through bleaching and dressing to packaging and despatch. From 500 workers at the site in 1876, the business grew to 1000 in 1886. In that same year a fire wrecked the buildings, followed by another six years later. The present building was erected between 1892 and 1893.

Wilkinson was as flamboyant as his factory. He had a gift for publicity and sent out one million 40-page booklets advertising his firm. The United States and Canada were very important outlets for his produce, and when overseas customers visited his works their na-

The Anglo-Scotian Mills

tional flag was flown from the "battlements". One New York order needed a special goods train to transport Wilkinson's curtains to Liverpool before being shipped across the Atlantic. Wilkinson ensured photographers were there to record the occasion. To Beestonians he was known simply as "FW".

Wilkinson died in 1897 and his business went into liquidation the following year. John Pollard then bought the business and turned it into tenement factories. Ariel Pressings now occupies this Grade II listed building.

5. Bingham

The Thomas Hardy of the Midlands

Grid Reference: 705396

Directions: Bingham is 10 miles east of Nottingham. There is free parking in the Market Place. From there walk down Market Street to Long Acre. Fisher Lane is on the opposite side slightly to the left, and Lushai Cottage is on the left towards the end of the street.

Lushai Cottage was for a time the home of James Prior Kirk, the writer who simply used the pen name James Prior. He was born on 9 September 1851 and has been described as the Thomas Hardy of the Midlands. The epithet is perhaps an exaggeration, but like Hardy, Prior set his novels in his native county, often using easily recognisable fictitious place names.

Prior was the son of a straw hat manufacturer. Like many young men at the time and in a similar position, he was destined for the legal profession. After three years, though, he abandoned his studies in favour of other occupations: teaching, farming and working for his father. Later, after a few abortive early efforts, he became a full-time writer.

With the cousin he had married in 1886, Prior moved to Bingham in 1891, staying there until his death. Whereas he had previously concentrated on stories and plays, he now began to write novels. Up to 1910 he wrote six of them: *Renie, Ripple and Flood, Forest Folk, Hyssop, A Walking Gentleman* and *Fortuna Chance*. As a novelist, Prior gained a good critical reputation.

Prior is most noted for *Forest Folk*, which contains many descriptions of the countryside around Blidworth, including Oxton, Mansfield, Sutton-in-Ashfield and Newstead. The story concerns two very different families, the Skrenes and the Rideouts, and is set in the Luddite era – the first half of the 19th century. Protagonist Tant Rideout is based on Blidworth hero Matthew Clay, famous for his heroism at Waterloo. Prior sometimes used the real names of people who existed, and in *Forest Folk* James Towle of Basford, who was hanged in 1814 following a Luddite incident, receives a mention. Prior's use of the Nottingham idiom is another interesting feature of the book. A pub in the village is called the *Forest Folk* and contains a stained glass window dedicated to the writer.

Prior died on 19 December 1922, and seems never to have received the recognition he deserved. Perhaps it is time for a reappraisal.

Lushai Cottage, where James Prior lived

6. Blidworth

A remnant from the Ice Age

Grid Reference: 579558

Directions: Heading east towards the village centre, turn left off the Main Street into Ricket Lane. Take the footpath to the left and follow the yellow markers for about 1200 metres. The boulder is in a field on the right.

The huge stone in a field called Rock Close in Blidworth is some-times referred to as the "Blidworth Boulder", sometimes the "Druids' Stone". A number of other glacial deposits of the kind were left in this area of Blidworth during the Ice Age, but this is the only survival. So as not to hinder cultivation of the fields, the other smaller ones were blown up and the remains removed. It is said to have Druidic connections, although there is no evidence of this – superstitions

The Druids' Stone

inevitably form over the years, and it no doubt adds romance to the village's name.

The stone is a mass of clay and gravel, flat-topped, over 4 metres high and 8 metres in circumference. Towards the base is a large hole through which, early in the 20th century, children were passed to cure their whooping-cough. It is mentioned in James Prior's novel *Fortuna Chance*.

A different kind of rock, known as Slaney's Stone, used to stand in Chapel Lane. The name comes from John Slaney, who had a farm in Kighill and frequently drank too much at the Little John in Fishpool. On 24 January 1893, the landlord put the drunken Slaney in his cart ready for his horse to take him home. He never got there, though: Slaney fell and was killed at the age of 72. The stone marked the spot where he was found, and stood about 200 metres north of Church Drive in Chapel Lane.

7. Blidworth

A cross and a church rebuilt

Grid Reference: 592559

Directions: The cross faces Blidworth Church south porch, 20 metres away. The church remains are in the churchyard.

A rare surviving old custom in Nottinghamshire is the Rocking Ceremony at Blidworth. This involved taking the male child baptised nearest to the first Sunday in February and rocking him in a cradle laden with flowers; the child was then paraded down the street in a carnival atmosphere. It became a time for family reunions but often rekindled old feuds, sometimes degenerating into violence.

Tom Leake was killed one Rocking Day for different reasons, though. He was the forest ranger besotted by the landlady's daughter at the Archer, a pub of low repute. The jealous Captain Salmon of Salterford Hall killed the 60-year-old Leake in a duel in 1597 and a cross was erected where Leake fell. The cross disintegrated in 1751 and the remaining base was moved to the church. When the church was to be

The remains of the previous church

rebuilt in 1839, Mrs Need of Fountain Dale salvaged both the cross and parts of the medieval church – windows, coffin slabs and a doorway – which would doubtless have otherwise been thrown away as rubble. She was responsible for the cross being rebuilt.

When Newstead Colliery Company bought Fountain Dale at the beginning of the 20th century, the incumbent vicar Revd R.H. Whitworth ensured that Tom Leake's cross was moved back to the churchyard. He also took back the pieces of the medieval church and G. Wells of Caunton erected them, following no particular plans.

About 100 years after the discontinuation of the Rocking Ceremony due to excesses of the participants, it was reintroduced in a more moderate form in 1922.

8. Blyth

Doom preserved

Grid Reference: 624873

Directions: Blyth is 6 miles north-west of Worksop. The church is in the village, near the junction of Sheffield Road and the B6045.

In 1088, Roger de Builli and his wife Muriel founded Blyth Priory Church. Building on it probably began immediately. Shortly before 1400 there was a conflict between the parishioners and the monks, as a consequence of which the east wall was built to create a division between the priory and the church. The Doom Painting was executed on the wall partly as adornment, partly to give a pictorial education to a largely illiterate congregation.

Up to 8 metres tall and 7 metres wide, the Doom Painting was probably done by an itinerant artist. It depicts the Last Judgement, with naked individuals coming out of coffins and Christ sitting above on a throne.

A lofty view of the Doom Painting

For four and a half centuries the painting lay hidden beneath a lime wash, which fortunately acted as a preservative. Then in 1703, a marble monument to Edward Mellish of Blyth Hall was put against the east wall, only to be carried to the north aisle in 1885. It was at the time thought that there were traces of the painting remaining, although nothing was done to verify this.

In 1987 cleaning and restoration began for the 900th anniversary of the church. It became evident that much of the painting was intact, but the area that had stood at the back of the Mellish sculpture was completely obliterated. The restoration work on the painting will last at least another 200 years, although it is impossible to see it exactly in its former glory: the vividly-coloured image the parishioners once saw has now faded. Blyth Church is normally open.

9. Bothamsall

The mystery castle

Grid Reference: 671732

Directions: Bothamsall is 6 miles north-west of Tuxford. The castle mound is in Netherfield Lane, about a quarter of a mile west of the village.

The man-made mound just outside Bothamsall village (pronounced "bottomzal" locally) on the north bank of the River Meden is called "Bothamsall Castle" by the villagers. These are certainly castle remains, although the speculation about it has been so great because we have no evidence of this as such. Because the earthworks are not as extensive or as well preserved as those at Laxton (*q.v.*) or Egmanton, there have been theories among historians that this is a Saxon "moot hill" for meetings of the wapentake of Bassetlaw, similar to the Tynwald Hill where the parliament met on the Isle of Man. Since historians had discovered where other districts in the county met – Bingham, Broxtowe, Newark and Rushcliffe – it seemed that this was an exciting find just waiting to be discovered. The mound did not appear to bear many features similar to other castles, and it was compared to similar earthworks just on the edge of the village of

Bothamsall

Burgh-le-Marsh in Lincolnshire. But by the 1950s it became generally accepted that this mound was indeed part of a motte (mound) and bailey (outer court) castle (see Laxton). There is a dry moat around it.

Until relatively recently the mound at Bothamsall, like others at East Bridgford and Car Colston, for example, was the site of Shrove Tuesday games.

10. Brinsley

When coal was king

Grid Reference: 465486

Directions: The headstocks at Brinsley are 1 mile north of Eastwood. There is a car park east of Mansfield Road by the Brinsley Lodge pub. Follow the footpath for 150 metres.

When D.H. Lawrence's father was a miner at Brinsley Colliery, Barber, Walker & Co were the owners. Lawrence famously used to collect his father's pay from a building that is still standing. Of the colliery itself, however, only the headstocks remain. A boiler and winding engine stood to the right of them, with railway tracks on the left. Over this was a screening plant where the coal would be put into size and quality order and then dropped through onto wagons below. Once they were full, the wagons would pass to the mineral railway line and join the main Langley Mill line. The footpath here is on the track of the old railway line.

Horses and ponies were used throughout the history of Brinsley Colliery. The animals were stabled underground and came out only briefly during the summer. In 1907 there were 47 of them in use at the colliery. In the first part of the 19th century, children, often under 10, would work for up to 14 hours in mines. Where sections of the mine were too low for the horses and ponies, children would pull the wagons with a belt fastened to their waists. In 1843 a minimum age of 10 was set for underground juvenile work, this being increased to 13 in 1877.

On 10 June 1883, two years before Lawrence's birth, there was an explosion at the colliery in which two men – William Dunn, an ostler, and Charles Wright, a labourer – lost their lives. 14 horses were also killed. The accident left an indelible impression on the community, strong enough for Lawrence to incorporate the incident into an early fictitious work of his: *The Odour of Chrysanthemums*.

In 1930 the colliery ceased production, but the shafts were left open until 1970 for the miners to access nearby collieries. The headstocks were preserved as an important feature of mining history and moved to the National Mining Museum at Lound in Bassetlaw. On

The headstocks back in their original place

the closure of the museum, they were moved back to Brinsley where they now form part of a picnic area. Note the small building on your left as you return to the car park. This is Vine Cottage, former home of Lawrence's Aunt Polly, whose husband met his death in a mining accident. She features prominently in *The Odour of Chrysanthemums*.

11. Budby

The workers' village

Grid Reference: 617700

Directions: Budby is 2 miles north-west of Ollerton on the west side of Worksop Road (the A616).

In a delightful setting, with the River Meden running by the road, the village of Budby was created by the first Earl Manvers specifically for housing the workers of the Thoresby estate. William Wilkins built it in 1807. He also built a school, where Earl Manvers' wife paid for the education and clothing of 18 poor girls, under a woody hill at the south-west extremity of Thoresby Park. The estate had 26 houses in a vaguely Swiss or Gothic Revival style, all with impressive gardens. In 1841 the population was 138.

An interesting feature of some of the houses is a two-storey porch with three-arched entrances in a semi-circle. These bear such a resemblance to the Earl Manvers pub at Radcliffe-on-Trent that the same architect must have been responsible. The unremarkable church at Budby, described by one writer as of the "tin tabernacle" kind, was demolished in 1969.

Nearby is Budby Castle, previously known as Castle William. It was built about 1789 by Carr of York for the clerk of works of the estate as both a house and a folly.

The village street with its hexagonal letter box

12. Bunny

The wrestling mathematician

Grid Reference: 583296

Directions: Bunny is 7 miles south of Nottingham. The entrance to Bunny Church is in Main Street, west of Loughborough Road.

In the north aisle of Bunny Church is an unusual statue depicting a highly unusual person. Sir Thomas Parkyns, known affectionately as "the wrestling baronet", greets the visitor with a wrestling stance. But Parkyns was not just an eccentric member of the aristocracy: he was the benefactor of Bunny and Bradmore and built a large number of the houses there.

The baronet (1662 to 1741) was educated at Westminster and Trinity College, Cambridge. As was the tradition in noble circles, he continued for some time at Gray's Inn. This was supposed more to build character than to prepare the young aristocracy for the Bar.

It would probably be easier to list what Parkyns did not build in the area than what he did, but he rebuilt Bunny Hall and put a wall round the park; inscribed the hall tower with his coat of arms; designed the school and almshouses on the main road; rebuilt many farmhouses; and he re-roofed the church chancel and donated two treble bells. His love of Latin is evident from the buildings in the area bearing his Latin inscriptions.

As a Justice of the Peace, Parkyns noted that the County Hall in Nottingham was unsafe, but objected to a future suggestion that the County Hall and gaol be moved to the Market Square. As a philanthropist, Parkyns had bread worth 5s 4d (26p) annually distributed to poor widows and widowers in Bunny and Bradmore.

It is certainly his passion for wrestling, however, for which he seems most noted. He wrote a book, *The Cornish Hugg Wrestler*, trained servants and neighbours in the sport and began a village custom which lasted over 90 years – an annual wrestling match on Midsummer's Day. In the early days he personally competed in the match. This began in 1712, with the first prize a gold-laced hat worth 22 shillings (£1.10) and the second prize just three shillings (15p). The last year of the custom was in 1810. The previous year there had been only two entrants, after which Lord Rancliffe announced that there would be no prizes the next year, and perhaps not surprisingly there were no entrants at all. Parkyns's book describes such exotic wrestling mysteries as the hanging trippet, the pinnion and the gripe.

Although the church is normally locked, inside the south porch is a list of nearby addresses where the key to the north porch can be borrowed.

Parkyns frozen in a proud wrestling position

13. Carburton

The tiny church

Grid Reference: 612733

Directions: Carburton Church is 4 miles north-west of Ollerton and off the Ollerton road (B6034). Turn right towards Clumber Park opposite the Old School House tea-rooms, then left into Piper Lane after 500 metres.

It is very easy to miss Carburton while driving along the main road or turning in to Clumber Park. When this tiny village's population peaked in 1853 it stood at 200. The church is equally minute, being one of the smallest in England, with seating for only 60 people. The appearance of the church is deceptive: from its stuccoed exterior it is hardly possible to tell that this is, in fact, an early 12th century building. A chancel, nave and square bellcote are all it consists of, with three stained glass windows commemorating F.J.S. Foljambe's wife. There is a sundial above the porch .

The Norman church

Perhaps the most interesting thing about Carburton Church is its register, even if it *is* no longer kept here. This dates back to 1528, and although it shares this distinction with neighbouring Perlethorpe and Elsworth in Cambridgeshire, no other churches in the country can boast the same. The date precedes by ten years Thomas Cromwell's pronouncement that registers of weddings, christenings and burials should be recorded. Also of note is the bell-shaped Elizabethan silver communion cup dating from 1571. The first Duke of Newcastle's equerry, John Mazine, has a memorial near the altar, and Manor Farm in the village was built for him. The church is normally open.

14. Car Colston

Free rent on the green

Grid Reference: 717427

Directions: Car Colston is off the A46, 8 miles south of Newark.

The first thing that strikes the visitor to Car Colston is the huge village green. At over 6.5 hectares it is one of the biggest in Europe and has an extremely long history. Lands were generally enclosed between 1750 and 1820 by act of Parliament. In some places, however, freeholders decided by mutual agreement how land should be enclosed, as was the case here, but at the very early date of 1598. It was also thought proper for smaller property owners to have some land in common. To this effect the green in the village remained the common property of surrounding cottagers, for grazing their animals, and the number of "owners" in 1845 was 24.

There are, in fact, two greens, sometimes referred to as Large Green and Little Green, the latter being approximately one third the size of the other. In the 1820s squatters erected two cottages around Large Green. The parish allowed them to do this, and even let them have their own enclosed gardens, for the nominal payment of one shilling (5p) per year. The argument in favour of this apparent charity was that it kept them off the poor rate. The parish constable failed to collect this nominal payment for a number of years, however, and an attempt to reimpose the fee failed because too much time had elapsed.

Animals usually grazed on the green in summer, and gates were used – at Tenman Lane, Scarrington Lane and near Screveton Church – until motorists became a nuisance by damaging them or not shutting them. The gates were taken down in 1929. A square pinfold stood on the green until it became so ruinous by 1850 that the pinfold at Screveton had to be used in its place until about the 1890s. Village stocks were also used for flogging criminals. Consisting of one pole, manacles and anklets, this was knocked down by a carthorse in World War II but subsequently restored. The cricket pavilion is now a more soothing sight on the green.

A large number of occurrences are associated with the green, such as the assembly of dissenters forming there in 1818 and a group of Chartists meeting in 1848. Up to World War I there was a fair held on Feast Day, the third Saturday in June. The custom was revived in the second half of the 20th century and is still recognised. The green retains its mystique for anyone visiting Car Colston, and some remains of the gates still exist.

The vast expanse of Large Green

15. Carlton

The short-lived brewery

Grid Reference: 616414

Directions: Carlton is 3 miles east of Nottingham. At Carlton Square, where Carlton Road becomes Burton Road, turn into Station Road then take the fourth right into Mar Hill Road. The former brewery is on the left on the corner of Primrose Street.

V ery little is known about Mar Hill Brewery, but bearing in mind its very short existence and its absence from any literature on local brewing history, it must have been a very unsuccessful undertaking. It was designed by Watson Fothergill in 1899 with 16 workers' cottages, and became a brewery in 1904. Willam Vickers, a previous licensee of the nearby Black's Head, ran it for less than three years.

It shows many of the hallmarks of the architect. Fothergill was Nottingham's second most famous 19th century architect next to Thomas Chambers Hine, but arguably its most interesting. Born

Mar Hill Brewery

Fothergill Watson in Mansfield on 12 July 1841, he was influenced by
Gothic architecture at an early age. This style was to be an important
feature of Fothergill's buildings, which are often a feast for the eyes
with their stone and wooden figures, tall chimneys, turrets and sad-
dlebacks. Mar Hill Brewery remains subdued compared with some of
the creations of the architect, who inverted his name in the 1880s.

Although Nottingham lost the Black Boy Hotel in Smithy Row to a
faceless sixties building, many of Fothergill's buildings still delight
those who look above ground level. A few of the most noteworthy are:
the Rose of England (now the Filly and Firkin) in Mansfield Road;
Queen's Chambers on the corner of Long Row and Queen's Street; the
Nottingham and Notts Bank (now the National Westminster) in Thur-
land Street, with its Portland stone friezes; and perhaps the most interesting, his former offices at 15 George Street, crammed with detail.
His influences included Pugin, Scott and Norman Shaw. The cityscape of Nottingham and its surrounding area would be much less
impressive without Watson Fothergill's architectural legacy.

After its death as a brewery, the building was put to several uses:
laundry and dye works, stocking factory, print works and it is now an
electronics company. The tower was damaged by fire some time ago.

16. Carlton-on-Trent

The gravel house

Grid Reference: 802642

Directions: Carlton-on-Trent is 7 miles north of Newark. Turn into the road
towards the River Trent, past Carlton Lane on the left and Teal's is just beyond
the car parking area.

The soil in Carlton-on-Trent is a sandy loam and clay. The pebbly
building by the River Trent was once the business of Robert Teal,
a sand and gravel merchant and dealer in road materials. Though not
listed in the 1894 trade directories, his name appears from the beginning of the 20th century. In 1932 he advertised crushed, washed and

Robert Teal's Trent gravel works

graded gravel of all sizes. By 1941 he had three other branches: Sutton-on-Trent, Nottinghamshire; Whisby near Lincoln; and North Hykeham just south of Lincoln. A little further up the lane is Carlton-on-Trent Windmill.

17. Church Warsop

The troubled watermill

Grid Reference: 569685

Directions: The watermill is north of Warsop on the east side of Church Road going towards Cuckney.

Warsop watermill is in a more picturesque part of the village opposite the mill dam and the Carrs (former marshlands). This listed building dates from 1825, was gutted by fire in 1922 but rebuilt in 1924. The waterwheel was used with a water turbine until 1946 when the mill was converted to electricity and the wheel removed.

The mill has been beset by problems throughout its history. Flooding used to be a constant threat, and then in the 1930s Staveley Coal & Iron Company caused subsidence. (The church suffered bigger problems and up to 1957 was supported internally and externally by a huge cradle.) The mill is still working and sells its own flour.

Warsop Watermill

18. Clayworth

The unhappy history of the Chesterfield Canal

Grid Reference: 732876 (Clayworth Bridge)

Directions: Clayworth is 6 miles north of Retford. Take the A620 out of Retford and continue along the B1403 into Hayton. The canal is at the south entrance to the village.

The Retford and Worksop Boat Club at the side of Clayworth Bridge was built in the 1930s to replace a wooden one. It used to be a pub called the White Hind. Also of interest in the village is a huge boulder in the church wall. One legend claims that navvies working on the canal in the 1770s found this and built it into the church wall on the death of one of their workmates while working on the canal.

The Chesterfield Canal stretches from Chesterfield in Derbyshire to West Stockwith in Nottinghamshire. It runs through Worksop and

The peaceful Chesterfield Canal (Otter's Bridge)

Retford and is 46 miles long in total, with 65 locks. In Nottingham-shire, where it is now fully navigable, it is 26 miles long. The water-way took six years to build and was completed in 1777. As one of the first canals to be built in England, the Chesterfield shows its age by winding considerably through its course: canals as a rule are straight.

The original survey was made by canal engineer James Brindley, who at a public meeting at the Red Lion* in Worksop revealed the cost the project. At the time, industrial produce from Chesterfield and rock from the quarries of Derbyshire travelled by road and river (the Idle) to the Trent – a long and sometimes difficult process. A canal would transform local industry, it was thought.

Brindley died in 1772, a year after work had begun, and it was eventually decided that his brother-in-law Hugh Henshall should take over. The stretch from Retford to Stockwith was widened to make allowance for the larger boats on the Trent. On 4 July 1777 the canal was finally completed and the first boat from West Stockwith arrived in Chesterfield.

The Chesterfield Canal was seen as a great provider of prosperity to the area and there were many celebrations. But there were prob-lems from the start and its history is full of financial difficulties and neglect. The roof of the Norwood Tunnel was damaged due to people digging for coal over it, and subsidence was a continual problem. The American War of Independence led to recession, reducing canal traf-fic and consequently tolls. A certain amount of money was coming in, but Chesterfield was hardly one of the most successful canals. Some of the lack of interest may have been because the canal had no junc-tions, no way of connecting to other canals. By the 1840s railways had arrived to bring a more efficient and faster form of transport. After a series of complicated mergers with railway companies, the Chester-field Canal lay neglected and underused.

In 1908 the Norwood Tunnel collapsed, ending commercial traffic beyond Shireoaks. After World War II there was no more coal-carrying, and in 1955 the transport of bricks from Walkeringham ceased. The last commercial traffic was in 1962, but volunteer groups have since applied their energies towards restoration. The aim is to have a fully navigable canal. The Chesterfield Canal is thought by many people to be one of Nottinghamshire's best kept secrets.

---

* This pub was in Victoria Square and later became the Golden Ball.

19. Clifton
The deceptive TIL house

Grid Reference: 544350

Directions: Clifton is 4 miles south-west of Nottingham. The TIL house is off Clifton Lane, 400 metres along Village Road.

The letters "L", "T", and "I" and the date "1707" are clearly visible in relief in the brickwork of the TIL house at 56 Village Road. It is believed the letters stand for Thomas and John (or Jane) Lambert, the owners at that date. This does not represent the date the house was built, but when the brick exterior was created. The house is in reality a wattle and daub cottage dating perhaps from the 14th century. As a building in the cruck style, the house has a pair of curved timber supports; at the time, all but the grandest domestic houses were built in this way. Brick only began to be used – and even then only by the rich – following the peace after the Wars of the Roses in 1485.

In 1966 Sidney Bradbury, a 75-year-old Gotham thatcher who had repaired the building 30 years previously, was hauled out of retirement to provide the same service. The fact that thatchers were in short supply was not the only problem – new harvesting methods meant there was difficulty finding straw long enough to do the job.

The thatched TIL house – older than it says

20. Clumber Park
The lake and surroundings

Grid Reference: 621738 (Clumber Bridge)

Directions: Take the Ollerton road (B6034) north of Budby – the same route as Carburton – and turn right opposite the Old School House tea-rooms into a road leading to the park. The bridge is visible on entering Lime Tree Avenue via Carburton Lodge.

One of the most attractive parts of Clumber Park is the lake. Extending 32 hectares, it was built over a period of 15 years, beginning 1772, at a cost of £6612. The River Poulter was dammed in the process. From the bridge in the west to the dam in the east the distance is 1.5 miles. Until the 1930s a small chain ferry was used to cross it. There was a cable on both banks and the remains of the winches can still be seen. Boats were once a feature here and in the early 1800s the Duke of Newcastle employed a sailor on the lake.

Reflections of a classical age

There was a resident model frigate called *The Lincoln*, although it caught fire and sank to the bottom during World War II. Some of the wood is at times still visible.

Opposite the church, on the south side of the lake and on the edge of the Boat House Plantation, is a Doric temple built of Steetley stone.

But perhaps the most interesting attraction of the lake is the classical bridge spanning its narrowest point. Standing between the River Poulter and the lake, Clumber Bridge was built by Stephen Wright in 1770, at the same time as Clumber House (largely rebuilt in the 19th century but demolished in 1938), the lodges and the temple. The bridge is in pale ashlar stone and has three almost semi-circular arches.

Clumber Park is owned by the National Trust and there is a car parking fee.

21. Cuckney

The mill workers' street

Grid Reference: 564713

Directions: Cuckney is 7 miles north of Mansfield. Ten Row is in Creswell Road, west of the Mansfield Road (A60).

Today Cuckney is divided in two by the Mansfield to Worksop road; the eastern half contains the church and the pub, and the western half the former mills and the mill workers' cottages. The mills employed children from all over the country, although a significant number came from the London Foundling Hospital. The orphans worked 12 hours a day from as young as seven, and at 14 were apprenticed, transferred to other mills or allowed to go. Some may have seen this as a merciful release: six per cent of them died before reaching 14, some through suicide.

The original mill first manufactured worsteds, with cotton goods produced at a later date. It was built in 1723 near the upper dam and was owned by a man called Toplis. The mill worked for well over a hundred years before becoming a school, as it is today. The top floor, which used to house some of the workers, has been demolished. Another mill in the same part of the village was Gorton's Mill which burned down in 1792. A third mill in the eastern half of the village also belonged to Toplis known as Lower Mill, was pulled down in the 1960s and a house built in its place.

Creswell Road was called Ten Row and was a street of ten terraced cottages designed to accommodate young mill workers. The houses were split into smaller units inside, segregated by gender and watched over by superintendents. The terrace was later extended, although two dwellings were destroyed in the second half of the 20th century to make way for road widening.

A few of Ten Row's cottages

22. Cuckney
The tree with the hole

Grid Reference: 566713

Directions: The Greendale Oak pub is on the corner of the A616 and Norton Lane, 200 metres south of the church.

The Greendale Oak tree used to stand in Welbeck Park, 700 metres south of the abbey. It is remembered in two pub names: this one at Cuckney and a lesser-known local in Norfolk Street, Worksop. The reason for its fame in the beginning was because it was so huge and so old – nicknamed "The Methuselah of the Forest", the tree is said to have been any-where from 16 to 27 metres high and capable of sheltering 225 cattle. Time is a great exaggerator, but the tree must still have been a colossal struc-ture. The age of it is also in dispute: some sources claimed 700 years in the 18th century, al-though the histo-rian Throsby more than dou-bled that. What-ever the age, by 1664 the tree was

An artists's impression of the Greendale Oak

clearly showing signs of age. This situation was worsened on 26 November 1703. During gales called the "great storm", when Eddystone Light was destroyed, thousands of trees were uprooted and the Greendale Oak lost some branches.

It is neither for its antiquity nor its size, however, that the Greendale Oak is so well known, but for the huge archway cut through it in 1724. The height of this was over three metres and a carriage and two horses could be driven through it. The reason for the vandalism was a bet made between the first Duke of Portland and the Earl of Oxford. The Countess of Oxford had a cabinet made with the cut wood, with engraved panels depicting the tree.

The Greendale Oak deteriorated rapidly and was for some time propped up with sticks and chains to hold the branches. It eventually became just a pile of old wood.

23. Daybrook

The Morleys at work

Grid Reference: 580447

Directions: Follow the Mansfield Road north of Nottingham until you see a sign to Arnold about 3 miles from the centre. The factory is at the junction of Mansfield Road and Nottingham Road.

John and Richard Morley were born at Sneinton Manor in the second half of the 18th century. The sons of a hosiery worker, they set up a firm known as J (usually "I") & R Morley in Greyhound Yard, Nottingham. John left for London to establish a bigger outlet for the sale of their goods, and it was there that Samuel, John's youngest son, was born on 15 October 1809.

Samuel Morley started working at the London business in 1825, and by 1860 was in total control of I & R Morley. Morley threw himself into his four concerns: business, philanthropic work, religion and politics. He was well respected by his employees and established one of the first pension funds for them.

Morley built a group of hosiery factories in Sneinton, Loughborough, Leicester, Heanor, Sutton-in-Ashfield and Daybrook. This factory still has the original name of the firm – "I & R Morley" – inscribed near the top in large letters. The building was bought by the Hardys in 1885, a year before Morley's death on 5 September 1886.

Samuel Morley's statue stood in Theatre Square from 1888 to 1927. It was smashed in the process of being moved to the arboretum entrance, and a bronze bust of the man was placed there instead. The Daybrook factory was extended in 1911.

Samuel Morley's factory

24. Drakeholes

Sentinels of the past

Grid Reference: 706904

Directions: Drakeholes is off the Gainsborough road (A631), 1 mile east of Everton. The Wiseton Hall lodge houses are above the Chesterfield Canal tunnel, opposite the Griff Inn.

Once the entrance to Wiseton Hall drive, the two derelict early 19th century lodge houses are a reminder of an aristocratic past. They were home for one family, one lodge being for living accommodation and the other to sleep in. There is an overgrown ice house nearby.

Jonathan Acklom of Wiseton Hall built the White Swan (now the Griff Inn) in the late 18th century. He also rebuilt Wiseton Hall and some new farms on the estate. Although nothing remains of the hall, some of the farms have survived intact.

The derelict lodge houses of Wiseton Hall

25. East Drayton
Church cheeses

Grid Reference: 775754

Directions: East Drayton church is in the centre of the village.

The belfry walls at the Church of St Peter at East Drayton are painted with a large number of red ochre rings. These represent cheeses given during marriage ceremonies in the 18th and 19th centuries. In the Middle Ages it was the custom for the banns to be read three times, the future bride and bridegroom standing in the church porch for identification. The church bells were rung at the end of the service. The cheese custom was a kind of revival of these times, the bells being rung with a special peal after the first service.

The church of St Peter

When this custom was practised, the bells were rung after the register was signed, and the ringing would continue intermittently throughout the day. After the first peal it was the custom for the bridegroom to go into the belfry with an enormous plum loaf and a whole cheese for the bell-ringers. After they had eaten their fill, the oldest bell-ringer would then give out the remaining food. He gave this to the children of school age, who would line up to enter the tower. The bell-ringers received £1 for their work and the money was always spent equally between the two village pubs, the Harrow Inn and the Bluebell Inn.* A last peal of bells was made at 6 o'clock the following morning. This custom was not unique to East Drayton – cheese rings were also painted at Treswell, Laneham and Egmanton over the same period – but it does appear to have been practised only in this area of Nottinghamshire.

There are nearly one hundred cheese rings on the church walls. The first was made in 1777 and the last 1865, with a single revival in 1891. They contain the first and last initials of the newlyweds, together with the date of marriage.

26. East Stoke

The US ambassador

Grid Reference: 754496

Directions: East Stoke is 4 miles south-west of Newark. The Pauncefote Arms is on the east side of the Fosse Way (A46) on the corner of Moor Lane. The church is in School Lane, left of the main road.

The Pauncefote Arms is listed as "Pensez Fort Arms" in some 19th century trade directories, although the original name was its present one. The earliest recorded date is 1808, 20 years before the birth of the most noted member of the Pauncefote family: Sir Julian.

---

* Only the Bluebell Inn still survives as a pub, the Harrow now being a private house.

The Pauncefote Arms, East Stoke

With all the interest in the Battle of East Stoke in 1487, it is easy to forget this other aspect of the village's history. Julian Pauncefote was born in Munich in 1828 and educated in England (Marlborough College), Paris and Geneva. He was called to the Bar in 1852. After three years practising law in Hong Kong he became Attorney-General of the former colony. Ten years later he was Chief Justice of the Leeward Islands, and on returning to England in 1874 continued his political rise.

It is for his diplomatic work in the United States that Pauncefote is most remembered. In 1889 he was appointed envoy there following the dismissal of Lord Sackville, who had been interfering with the elections. Relations between Britain and the United States were at a dangerously low ebb, but Pauncefote's skills greatly assisted in bridging the gulf between the two countries. Four years later he became ambassador. One of the most important disputes Pauncefote had to settle was open sea sealing by the Canadians in the Behring Sea. This was an argument that was eventually resolved amicably in 1892 at an arbitration tribunal in Paris. Another issue involved a border dispute between Venezuela and British Guyana, which was again settled in Paris.

But it is the war with the United States and Spain that most helped to secure the lasting friendship between Britain and North America. Here Pauncefote used his considerable ambassadorial skills to great effect. Not so many years previously this would have been considered impossible. John Hay was the US Secretary of State in 1901. Towards the end of that year the historic Hay-Pauncefote Treaty was signed. It gave the United States the right to build a canal connecting the Pacific to the Atlantic Ocean, with free passage of vessels from any country. Work on the canal began in 1902 and was completed in 1914. Pauncefote was by this time approaching the end of his life and on 24 May 1902 died in Washington. It is a measure of the respect that the Americans held for him that the president and other leading American figures attended his funeral. His body was sent back to England in the warship *The Brooklyn*, the flagship of the Flying Squadron. The coffin was draped with the American flag. Pauncefote was buried at St Oswald's Church at East Stoke and a bronze monument to this first and very important ambassador to the US stands at the head of the grave.

27. Edwinstowe

The chapel in the forest

Grid Reference: 596666

Directions: The chapel is 2 miles east of Market Warsop. Where Forest Road (the B6035) meets the Mansfield Road (A6075), make your way east towards Edwinstowe. Park in the second parking area on your left, just before the end of the forest. Take Clipstone Drive – an unmarked path – for 500 metres, then turn right into a less-trodden path. The cross is 400 metres on your right.

A few stones and a cross on the edge of Sherwood Forest mark the origins of Edwinstowe in the 7th century. St Edwin was the King of Northumbria – a land stretching from the River Trent to Edinburgh – and married Princess Ethelburga of Kent, the first Christian kingdom in the country. Aided by the persuasive powers of his wife, Edwin was converted to Christianity by Bishop Paulinus, whom

Edwinstowe – St Edwin's cross

Ethelburga had brought with her to York. Edwin then encouraged Paulinus's missionary activities in northern England. Along with Edwin, many members of his court were also converted to Christianity and baptised in AD625 on Easter Sunday. The place of Edwin's baptism was a small church in York – later to be rebuilt as York Minster – and the site is now marked in the crypt of the minster.

Edwin's enemy was King Penda of Mercia, and between 632 and 633 Edwin travelled south to meet him. A battle was fought at Heathfield – near either Doncaster or Cuckney – where Edwin was killed. His men gave him a secret Christian burial in the forest clearing and a small chapel was built on the spot. To honour his fight against the ungodly, Edwin was canonised. The name "Edwinstowe" means that this is Edwin's burial place. The chapel was in existence in King John's time – John paid a hermit to live there and pray for his soul and the souls of all those he had wronged. For centuries this was associated with the royal chapel at Clipstone Palace (see Old Clipstone). As a chantry chapel it came under King Henry VIII's ban. Stones from the chapel were found when excavations were made. They were placed around a central iron cross with a stone tablet giving a summary of the story.

28. Edwinstowe
Collecting words

Grid Reference: 625669

Directions: At the crossroads in the centre of Edwinstowe, the church is near the corner of Mansfield Road (A6075) and Church Street. Brewer's modest grave is sheltered by trees, 20 metres west of the tower.

Edwinstowe is the stopping-off place for visitors to Sherwood Forest hoping to retrace the footsteps of Robin Hood. A sign in the churchyard even notes the supposed wedding of the famous outlaw and Maid Marian. Far less known is the grave of Dr Ebenezer Cobham Brewer. This is the same Brewer who created the famous reference books, the most notable of which is *Brewer's Dictionary of Phrase and Fable.* Published in 1870 and still a major reference work, the dictionary has been updated – even slightly sanitised by political correctness – but the book retains the same marvellously old-fashioned quality as before.

Brewer's grave

Brewer was born on 2 May 1810 in Russell Square in London and educated at Trinity Hall, Cambridge. In 1835 he graduated with a first class honours degree in Civil Law, followed by a doctorate in 1840. He appears to have wanted a college fellowship because he was ordained a deacon and then a priest, but his ambitions seem to have been thwarted because he was later teaching at his father's school, Mile End House in Norwich.

After six years in Paris in

the 1850s, Brewer returned to England and married. By then he had gained a good reputation as a non-fiction writer. After the death of his wife in 1871, Brewer went to live with his eldest daughter and her husband, the Revd Henry Telford Hayman, at the Ruddington vicarage. In 1884 they moved to the vicarage at Edwinstowe. Brewer often wrote into the early hours of the morning and noted the names and dates of visitors on his bedroom walls. One of them was the beautiful Duchess of Portland, who sat on his bed while chatting to the old man.

Brewer died on 6 March 1897. His legacy is over 40 books, several of which were written in Nottinghamshire, such as: *The Smaller History of Germany* (1881), *A Dictionary of Miracles* (1884), *Authors and their Works* (1884) and *The Historic Notebook* (1891). But it is *A Dictionary of Phrase and Fable (New and Enlarged Edition)* for which he has become famous. This was completed between 1894 and 1895 and is his last work. In it, the reader is treated to a vast list of expressions, clichés and proper nouns that a conventional dictionary would not contain. "Thou shall not muzzle the ox when he treadeth out the corn" (rough translation: do not begrudge a person a few perks in life) and "a soft fire makes a sweet malt" – similar to the proverb "more haste less speed" – are just two examples of the gems contained in this unique work.

29. Elston

The bus company at the windmill

Grid Reference: 761476

Directions: Elston is 5 miles south of Newark. In Mill Road south of the village, Elston Windmill is on private property but clearly visible from the road.

Elston Windmill was erected in 1844, and on the day work began the sails fell down on top of a 14-year-old boy. The mill was in the Lee family until 1901, when it was sold to Colonel Darwin of Elston Hall.

The windmill was out of action for some years up to 1919 when the

Gash family took it over. William Gash senior was from Syerston, and when he made the purchase his son, William Gash junior, an engineer, had just returned from Tyneside after the depression in the aircraft industry. He moved into the property with his wife, Euphemia, and started selling animal foodstuffs. They were later joined by William's younger brother, Alan, and ran an additional mill at Long Bennington on the Lincolnshire border with Nottinghamshire.

At the mill the Gash family also ran the Elston Motor Service, later known as William Gash & Sons bus company. William had originally bought a second-hand Humber truck in 1921 and began carrying passengers on a small basis. At first the Gashes carried passengers to Newark Market only, but soon extended the service from Elston to Nottingham on Saturdays. A return to Broad Marsh was 4s 6d (22.5 pence). By 1928 there was a daily service from Elston to Newark in the Gashs' 14-seater buses. The company continued to expand over the years and moved to Newark in 1953. The business was taken over by Lincolnshire Roadcar in the late 1980s.

Meanwhile, the windmill flourished for a time. In 1940 the sails were taken off because they were interfering with Newton airfield. The Gashes, neverthe-

An example of a Gash bus

less, continued the milling business, using auxiliary power, well into the 1940s. The tower mill had a black ogee cap and was 15.5 metres tall. Now, minus its cap, it has been converted into a home and painted bluish-grey.

30. Farnsfield

Free board and lodging

Grid Reference: 645567

Directions: Farnsfield is 4 miles north-west of Southwell. The lock-up is on the west side of the village in Main Street. It is on the north side of the road, 100 metres before the narrow Chapel Lane branches off to the east.

In Farnsfield village there is a small building with a sheet of iron with holes for a window. This used to be the village lock-up, and this and the one in Tuxford* are the only remaining two in the county. The purpose of lock-ups was the temporary detainment of prisoners – they were never intended as long-term stay places. The buildings belonged to the parish and were the responsibility of the parish policeman, who was entrusted with the prisoners until they were sent for trial.

An anecdote has been passed down by 85-year-old villager George Stevens who died in 1938. He claimed that an old man was apprehended one evening for being in a terrible state after a long drinking session. The policeman thought it would be for the man's own good if he spent the night in the lock-up. The next morning the prisoner's wife brought him a time-honoured hangover cure: she filled a bowl with beer, lifted it to his cell window and passed a clay pipe through one of the holes for him to suck up the drink!

Lock-ups went out of use in the middle of the 19th century, victims of police stations with their own cells. Sometimes there are other

---

* The lock-up at Tuxford has an 1823 datestone and contains two cells, probably designed to segregate the sexes.

paraphernalia of punishment near a lock-up, such as stocks or whipping-posts. One surviving example of the latter is at Radcliffe-on-Trent.

The Lock-Up

31. Fledborough

Nottinghamshire's Gretna Green

Grid Reference: 812722

Directions: The tiny village of Fledborough is 8 miles east of Tuxford.

The foremost place for clandestine marriages is usually thought of as Gretna Green, but for some years in the 18th century, Fledborough served as a rival. The Revd William Sweetapple was the man responsible for this. He became vicar at the parish church in 1712, when there were 11 families here. At the beginning of his incumbency there were few marriage ceremonies, but by 1753 Sweetapple had married 490 couples, only 15 of whom lived in the parish.

As word of this Midlands Gretna Green spread, the number of marriage licences granted in Fledborough increased: 11 in 1731, 21 in 1740, 34 in 1749 and finally, 43 in 1753. Sweetapple had built his own parsonage and was obviously prospering on the proceeds of his

Where the Revd Sweetapple married eloping couples

sideline. He was able to get away with it for so long for a number of reasons. The fact that he was marrying individuals living outside the parish, doing so without banns and outside normal service hours was breaching only two minor canons. Sweetapple was a very quiet and undemonstrative person, and most people aware of what he was doing would hardly be likely to complain to the authorities. Finally, of course, Fledborough was in an isolated situation.

Sweetapple's fall came in 1754 with the passing of the "Act for the better preventing of Clandestine Marriages". He would not have had long to continue his services, however: he died in August 1755. In his time at least one nobleman, using an alias, is said to have been married by Sweetapple.

Fledborough Church now belongs to the Churches Conservation Trust, formerly the Redundant Churches Fund (see Saundby).

32. Gedling

The DIY Windmill

Grid Reference: 629427 (Gedling House)

Directions: Gedling House is a private dwelling and can be seen on the north side of the Burton Road (A612) between Gedling and Burton Joyce.

A fascinating painting of a smock windmill south-east of Gedling village shows Gedling House in the background. The mill has four common sails and seems to be vaguely hexagonal with a strange patchwork appearance. The most remarkable thing about it, though, is a long thin tree branch running from the ground to an opening at the back of the mill cap.

The *Nottingham Journal* of 24 October 1801 contained an advertisement inserted by a Zakariah Barratt of Gedling, in which he encouraged people to buy a kind of DIY mill which he called a "Family Mill". The public were invited to his house to see it, and the advertisement stated, "The above mill may be erected in gardens, crofts, or to the gable ends and corners of houses, barns, granaries, or wherever the wind may have access." The superior quality of the flour that the mill could produce was emphasised, as well as the lack of waste; Barratt also claimed that anyone could be an efficient miller after a few days' experience. Prices varied according to the size of the mill required.

In 1956 there was an exchange of letters between windmill experts H.E.S. Simmons and Paul Baker of Carlton, in which the latter expressed strong doubts about the effectiveness of the mill. Barratt was a cabinet-maker by trade, but had also invented a form of washing-machine and a chimney-cleaning machine. The tree branch was there to act as a very primitive kind of brake and Baker doubted if Barratt's invention had many – if any – takers.

The windmill is unfortunately long gone, although the private Gedling House, for a long time council property, is still there and clearly visible from the road.

Zakariah Barrett's idea of a windmill

33. Gonalston
The giant horseshoe

Grid Reference: 681474

Directions: On the Southwell road (A612) towards Southwell, take the second signposted turning on the left to Gonalston. The old smithy is 150 metres on the right.

The brick smithy in Gonalston village has an enormous horseshoe, also in brick but in relief and painted black, around its entrance. A datestone is marked "J F 1854". Near the top of the structure is a weather vane with a fox incorporated, and over the doorway is a poem redolent of a bygone era:

> Gentlemen as you pass by
> Pray on this shoe, cast your eye.
> If it is too tight, we'll make it wider:
> 'Twill ease the horse and please the rider.
> If lamely shoeing (as they sometimes are)
> You can have them eased with the greatest care.

The smithy is not unique, even in Nottinghamshire: there is a similar horseshoe at Carlton-on-Trent, Dunmore in Scotland and a stone horseshoe exists at Belton in Lincolnshire.

The old smithy

34. Gringley on the Hill
The mysterious Beacon Hill

Grid Reference: 743907

Directions: Gringley is 8 miles north of Retford. Approaching the village on the A631 from the west, turn left towards Walkeringham. Beacon Hill is on the corner of Beacon Hill Road and High Street.

The beacon built by blacksmith Jack Rennison

Beacon Hill is the highest ground for some distance around this area. Not a lot is known about it, archaeological surveys having proved fruitless. Roman relics have been found nearby, but no Roman occupation is known of. The hill is man-made and has been used for beacon fires for events of national and local importance. It was used for signalling purposes during the Napoleonic wars and has also been popular with radio buffs, but the purpose of its existence remains a mystery.

It was here that Prince Rupert is said to have camped when he beat the Parliamentarians and helped the Royalists in Newark Castle in 1644. Below the hill stands a large model of a beacon built by village blacksmith Jack Rennison (1915-1995) in 1988.

35. Haughton
The chapel in the park

Grid Reference: 691730

Directions: Only the foolhardy would attempt to find the chapel ruins in the summer: the footpath is then dense with vegetation and the walk is by no means short. On the B6387 there is a car parking area about 1 mile north of Walesby. The trek begins from here. Pass under the railway bridge and follow the River Maun beyond Haughton Hall Farm until you reach a copse where the ruins lie, partly strangled by plants. The journey is less than 1 mile – but seems much longer. Appropriate clothing and a dogged determination are essential!

There is no indication in the slight remains of St James's Chapel, or the surrounding area, of just how important Haughton was in the history of the county. It was in the 16th century that Haughton underwent great changes. Before that it had been just a small village owned for many generations by the Stanhope family, Haughton Chapel being the parish church.

When ownership of Haughton passed to Edward Stanhope in 1509, however, things moved fast. He depopulated the village in or-

Haughton chapel ruins

der to create a vast, enclosed park to rear animals for hunting. Haughton Chapel was included in these 97 hectares, effectively becoming the domestic chapel of the Stanhopes.

Haughton estate was later sold to William Holles by Stanhope's daughter, Saunchia, and her husband, John Babington. It was William Holles, the son of the Lord Mayor of London of the same name, who built a large part of Haughton Hall after his father died. He was a man of great wealth and known as "Good Sir William". Haughton became the finest house in the county, Holles sparing no expense and even employing his own company of actors to keep him amused when he so desired. He died in 1590 and was buried in the chapel.

It was not until the 18th century that Haughton changed hands from the Holles family to the Dukes of Newcastle, and when Clumber was built in 1770 Newcastle destroyed Haughton Hall. Apart from the chapel remains, some of which date from Norman times, there are only the names Decoy House and Haughton Decoy to the south-west – after the duck decoy pond in Stanhope's park – to serve as any reminder of the greatness of Haughton. The site of the hall is now occupied by a farmhouse.

36. Hickling
The school that had to close

Grid Reference: 692285

Directions: Hickling is 12 miles south-east of Nottingham. Hickling School is on the east side of Main Street.

Hickling National School opened in 1837 to cater for 80 pupils. On 3 December 1873 the parish applied to the Board of Education to build a new school. This was, in fact, an enlargement of the first and it opened on 20 November 1876 with 72 children in the morning and 78 in the afternoon – perhaps the reverse of what might occur today! The first headteachers of the newly-extended school were Mr and Mrs Wilkinson, who stayed there until 1902.

During the Edwardian period ownership of Hickling School passed to the council. From 1903 to 1911, J.L. Laws was headteacher.

The village hall, formerly the school

Jack Laws was an amateur artist who sketched a number of views of the village and surrounding area. He seemed particularly interested in windmills and did a few sketches of the old mill at Hickling. He once sent a watercolour of Plumtree Mill on a postcard to a friend, apologising for his poor handwriting as he had his son Eric on his knee.

An anonymous handwritten account entitled "Memories of a Villager" recalls the school bell that was rung vigorously at 11 o'clock every Shrove Tuesday. This was to remind mothers to prepare the pancake mixtures. Pancake Day was celebrated by a half-day off school,* when the children enjoyed playing with their whips and tops, marbles and shuttlecock and battledores. Empire Day, the writer continues, was also a highly memorable school day, when the union flag was hoisted and the school piano taken outside for the singing of Empire songs. The flag was saluted at the end.

---

* In Ruddington, at about the same time, the church school bell – the "Pancake Bell" – was rung on Shrove Tuesday to signal the afternoon holiday. Children walked up the Old Road (then called High Hill) to roll cheeses down the slopes and run after them. There was no competitive element to the activity and the custom was no longer observed after the 1930s.

The good times did not last, though. For some decades before closure, the school only had about 12 pupils on its register. It was decided in the 1960s to send those pupils to Harles Acres in Kinoulton.
In 1963 the Women's Institute protested vociferously and drew up a
petition which was signed by all the villagers. But the inevitable was
not far away. The school closed in 1966, its last headteacher being
Miss B.E. Hatton. The building is now a village hall.

37. Holme-by-Newark
Nan Scott's chamber

Grid Reference: 803591

Directions: Holme Church is off the A1133, 4 miles north of Newark. Follow
Holme Lane west of the A1133 for 1 mile.

A nn Scott, or Nan Scott as she is more frequently called, was a
widow living on her own in Holme in the 17th century. Her story
has no doubt been embroidered by time, but remains true in essence.
    In 1666 Nan Scott was understandably extremely concerned about

Nan Scott's room above the church porch

the plague sweeping the country: it had started in London and had now reached Newark. Knowing it would soon strike the village, she began stockpiling enough food and drink to last her a few weeks. She then bolted herself in a small room above the south porch of St Giles Church. She stayed there watching the events from her window, using an old chest in her room as a bed.

The small village grew even smaller when the plague ravaged. Nan watched as her friends were all buried. When her food ran out and she eventually emerged from her self-imposed imprisonment, there was only one other villager remaining. In a mixture of emotions, she went back to the chamber until her death. The room, accessed by a spiral staircase, still contains the chest.

38. Holme Pierrepont

The shrinking hall

Grid Reference: 626392

Directions: Holme Pierrepont Hall is 5 miles east of Nottingham. From Holme Pierrepont Country Park and National Water Sports Centre, continue along Adbolton Lane. A signpost on the left indicates the church and hall.

Holme Pierrepont Hall was built about 1510 for the Pierrepont family, whose descendants still own it today. The south front is original and one of the earliest brick buildings in the county.

In keeping with the fashion of the Restoration period, in 1628 Robert Pierrepont – the first Earl of Kingston – made enlargements and changed the layout of the garden. The mansion has attracted a large number of noteworthy people over the years, among them the poet John Oldham, a great friend of William Pierrepont, the second Earl of Kingston. Oldham died of smallpox at the hall in 1683; there is a monument to him, probably by Grinling Gibbons, in the church at the side of the hall.

In the 18th century the Pierreponts were using Thoresby Hall as their principal residence and as a result Holme Pierrepont Hall became redundant. This was why the second Duke of Kingston reduced the size of it in the 1730s. His wife was the beautiful and illiterate Elizabeth Chudleigh, who only visited the hall once because she objected to its closeness to the churchyard. Several years after the death of the duke she was convicted of bigamy with him: her first husband was Captain Hervey, whom she had secretly married 25 years before the duke. Her wish to be buried chained to the duke's coffin in Holme Pierrepont Church was not respected.

A bowling green was once very popular here and the "wicked Lord Byron" is said to have played bowls with William Chaworth, whom he killed in a duel in 1765. The poet Lord Byron is also thought to have paid a visit here. The building became a dower house, and when the dowager Countess Manvers lived here she had a special house built for her pet monkey.

By this time the impressive red brick building had been hidden beneath cement rendering since 1814. It was removed in 1971. The hall is open to visitors on Easter Sunday and summer bank holiday Sundays and Mondays from 14.00 to 18.00, and at the same times on Sundays in June and July. It is also open on Thursdays in July, and Tuesdays, Thursdays and Fridays in August – again at the same times. There is an admission charge.

The Tudor hall at Holme Pierrepont

39. Hucknall

The healer's monument

Grid Reference: 536485

Directions: Hucknall is 8 miles north of Nottingham. The entrance to Titchfield Park is in Park Drive. Take the second (smaller) entrance to Titchfield Park and the monument is right in front of you. Smith's cottage (a private dwelling) is at 204 Beardall Street.

A memorial fountain in Titchfield Park* is dedicated to the healer, Zakariah Green. It was originally erected in the Market Place – where it held pride of place – and can be seen in the background of many old postcards of Hucknall.

Green's father, Richard, caught the ague in one of the Napoleonic wars and was taken to a hospital in Antwerp. After he had recovered from his illness, he worked as a hospital orderly, helping the overworked doctors and greatly earning their respect. It is this gift of healing which Zakariah would inherit. He was born on 5 May 1817 at a house in the High Street, approximately opposite the Chequers Inn. His education was modest, being received from the parish clerk, John Woollatt, at Sunday School. Zakariah was, nevertheless, a keen learner, and the knowledge gained helped him later with his medicine and surgery. His parents moved to a cottage in Beardall Street in 1829. There his retired father worked at a stocking-frame, and also healed the sick. Zakariah assisted his father until his death in 1843.

Green cared for the cottage well following his father's death. He was particularly fond of his garden and enjoyed plants as much as study. Great numbers of people – rich and poor – flocked there for the benefit of his healing powers. Six successive mayors of Hucknall are said to have sought his help, as well as many notable people who are

---

* The Duke of Portland, to commemorate the coming of age of his son, the Marquis of Titchfield, gave 4.5 hectares of land to the town. In July 1922 the marquis opened Titchfield Park. The council added more land, as did the Hucknall Miners' Welfare Committee, and the park had tennis courts, a bowling green, a bandstand, tea-room, pavilion and shelters.

unnamed. Green married Mary Mellors in 1850 and attended the Baptist chapel where he played the bass fiddle. He was also a member of the Windmill Friendly Club which met initially at the Half Moon, then the Chequers and finally the Seven Stars, where the landlord built a large clubroom for the members.

At a public meeting in the National Schoolroom in 1865, a number of grateful people presented Green with a purse containing 45 guineas (£47.25). He later refused all offers to have his cottage renovated by public subscription.

After the death of his wife he lost much of his sense of purpose, although his son, Samuel Green, helped him out, latterly taking over the administration of the concern. Zakariah died on 22 January 1897 at the age of 79 and was buried in Hucknall churchyard. A Thomas Hardy – one of the contributors to the purse presented to Green – collected £400 for a permanent memorial to the man. The red and grey granite structure bears a portrait of Green on one side, with later additional inscriptions to his son Samuel and each of his two grandchildren on the other sides. The medallion is thought to be a very good likeness. Green's house in Beardall Street still stands.

Zakariah Green's monument in Titchfield Park

40. Hucknall

The library with the horse on top

Grid Reference: 533493

Directions: The library is in the centre of the town in the Market Place, by the entrance to the church.

Hucknall Free Library was given to the town in 1887 by John Edward Ellis and Herbert Byng Paget. It was built by A.N. Bromley at a cost of £2000. When it opened the library contained 5000 books, a large reading room, games and conversation rooms and accommodation for the librarian. Short evening lectures during the winter proved highly successful. Along with a penny rate, the Byron Society provided financial support for it in Edwardian times and the average daily number of readers was 500. It was managed by the Committee of District Councillors.

Ellis and Paget were noted benefactors. Following the deaths of

The history of the library

several partners in the Hucknall Colliery Company – among them William Paget of Sutton Bonington and Alfred Ellis of Leicester – the two public benefactors held sole ownership of the firm from 1880. The company was registered as a limited company in 1898, a large number of shareholders coming from the Ellis family.

We know far more about Ellis than we do his partner. John was born in Leicester in 1841 and was an enthusiastic Quaker who had spent some time studying railway methods in the United States. He arrived in Hucknall in 1861 to apply some of the ideas he had learned. At first a Conservative, he soon embraced Liberalism as a better medium for social change. He was well liked and was actively involved in the mining profession until about 1885.

From this date politics monopolised his professional life. One change he brought about as an MP was to end the practice of the House of Commons taking a day off for Derby Day. It seems ironic, then, to see a racehorse (Golden Miller) as a weathervane on the library. This was salvaged from the demolition of the stable block at Hucknall in the 1920s. Ellis died in 1910.

41. Hucknall

The Bendigo challenger

Grid Reference: 533494

Directions: Ben Caunt's memorial is in St Mary's churchyard, east of the church.

Bendigo has almost monopolised talk of 19th century boxing in Nottinghamshire, with little interest at all being shown in the champion fighter whose monument is in Hucknall Cemetery. Benjamin Caunt (1815-1861) was born in Hucknall and was the arch-rival of Bendigo. He was 1.81 metres tall and weighed 89 kilograms. A very sportsmanlike figure, Caunt's best fights were marathons with Bendigo, who was four years older. His first meeting with the man was in 1835, when Bendigo beat him in 22 rounds. Their next encounter was in 1838 on Skipworth Common near Selby. Bendigo had recently won the championship by defeating Bill Mooney after 99 rounds and a gruelling 1 hour 45 minutes. He was not so fortunate with Caunt, though. Bendigo was beaten in 76 rounds.

Bendigo was not satisfied with the verdict, however, and maintained that he had accidentally fallen in the last round. A third fight was eventually organised in 1845 for a purse of £200 and a championship belt. Caunt put up a very good fight, but after 93 rounds and 130 minutes a decision was made in favour of Bendigo.

Caunt died in 1861. His son erected the monument in memory of his father, sister Martha (aged eight) and brother Cornelius (aged six). Both children had died in a fire at Caunt's home in St Martin's Lane, London.

Big Ben at Westminster is normally thought to be named after the first Commissioner of Works, Sir Benjamin Hall. A point of interest is that some historians have suggested that big Ben Caunt is really the person after whom it was named. We shall probably never know the truth.

The memorial to Ben Caunt

42. Hyson Green

Nottingham's second citizen

Grid Reference: 556416

Directions: The Old General is on the south corner of Radford Road and Bobbers Mill Road.

The statue of the "Old General" in front of the pub of the same name commemorates one of Nottingham's greatest eccentrics. It was carved by mason Joseph Holmes in his open field studio close to Radford Road and was first put on show at Nottingham Castle Museum before being moved to a showroom in Radford Road. When Joseph's brother, John, built the Old General pub and became the landlord in 1883, the statue was taken to its present position.

Benjamin Mayo, usually called the Old General, was born in Nottingham about 1779. He had round shoulders, a very prominent forehead and was little more than 1.5 metres tall. His shirt was usually unbuttoned and his sparse hair generally without a hat, apart from when he turned 60 and began sporting a military cap. He was a regular churchgoer and considered himself the most important person in the town apart from the mayor. Although a lot called him dim-witted, he was by no means stupid, especially when finding ways of making people part with their money.

The Old General sold broadsheets, ballads and chap-books. On one occasion he ran through the streets crying that he had a copy of a grand and noble speech made by the Duke of York. When buyers challenged him on realising they had bought a blank sheet of paper, the Old General replied, "The duke said nowt!"

Mayo was a great favourite with children and behaved with them as he thought a general would. Mickleton Monday was the time when he was most popular. Then, hundreds of children would take a holiday and follow him around, visiting schools where teachers were not observing the occasion. Where this was the case, they tried to persuade the teachers or the children that this was not a day to be in school. He was usually successful. Sometimes, though, his army would break school windows with stones in their frustration with recalcitrant teachers.

Many other stories have been passed down about the Old General. One day he found a sixpence and on being asked for it by someone who thought it was theirs, Mayo asked if it had a hole in it. On being told it had, the Old General said, "This hasn't, so it's not yourn." Perhaps surprisingly, women are said to have admired this pauper. He always promised to marry them "next Sunday morning", adding that they had better not make it later than half past seven in the morning or someone else may have claimed him.

The Old General described his occupation as a "flying stationer" and lived in St Peter's Poor House until it closed. Then he lived at the master Hudson's house, and finally at the Union Workhouse in York Street. It was there that he fell and died shortly afterwards. He was buried at the Broad Marsh burial ground, although his friends put up a plaque on the wall of the General Cemetery.

There were once two other Old General pubs – in Cross Street and Wellington Street – and Mayo Road was also named after the man.

The Old General's statue above the entrance to the pub

43. Kimberley

The chapel on the hill

Grid Reference: 503444

Directions: Kimberley is 5 miles north-west of Nottingham. The chapel is off Nottingham Road at the end of Broomhill Road. It can also be reached by ascending a few steps in the far corner of the car park at Sainbury's.

The mortuary chapel and cemetery at Kimberley stand as prominent and picturesque features of the town. In 1448 the depopulated parish of Kimberley was united with Greasley until 1847. In that
year a new church – St Wilfred's – was built to cater for a new parish
that had grown on the strength of the brewing and lace industries. By
the 1880s, however, the cemetery was full. The largest landowner
was the lord of the manor, Earl Cowper, who donated a plot of land for
a new burial ground.

Richard Charles Sutton* of Nottingham built the chapel, a typical
Victorian structure of its kind, and it was completed on 7 November
1883. It cost £2700 and the first burial was that of a child a few days
later. Figures from both the original breweries, Hardy's and Hanson's,
are represented in the graveyard: William and Eleanor Hardy and
Robert Goodhall Hanson. Also buried there is Joseph Payne, who
built the Crich Stand Memorial, and Godfrey and Mary Bostock. The
last two lived in Edgeware Road in the village and met their deaths by
a train crossing the tracks at West Hallam. The husband was an em-
ployee of R.G. Hanson's.

A few notable events have occurred in the 20th century. In 1938
Cemetery Road, which leads up to the chapel, was renamed Broomhill Road – obviously more pleasant-sounding for anyone planning to
live on it. Then in the late 1950s, the bell turret was found to be unsafe, so following the architecturally uncaring spirit of the times, it
was taken down rather than repaired.

The chapel is lit at night to deter vandals: in the past the chapel

---

* Sutton also built the United Methodist Free Church at Kimberley in 1890.

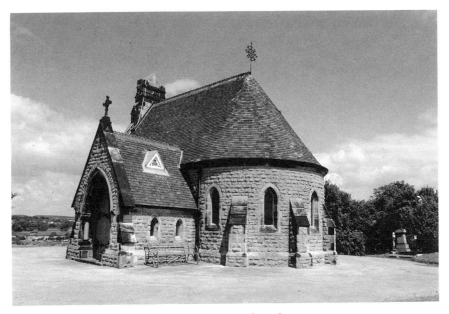

The mortuary chapel

was broken into and a book of remembrance removed from it, and a cast iron seat was taken from outside on another occasion.

44. Kingston-on-Soar

The Babington Plot

Grid Reference: 502277

Directions: Kingston-on-Soar is 10 miles south of Nottingham and the Babington Monument is in the chancel at St Winifred's.

Inside the late Victorian church of St Winifred's is an elaborate chantry chapel built by the Babington family in the first half of the 16th century. Such chapels were for many years used by the rich as a kind of spiritual insurance policy: a priest would be paid to sing for the souls of the dead members of the family and related families. Sir

The magnificent Babington monument

Anthony Babington had begun work on the monument at the same time as an earlier church, and following his death in 1536, his wife continued his work. Her son, John, finished it in 1538, a year after her death.

The monument consists of a canopy supported by four columns covered with hexagonal shapes. All over the capitals are a rebus (a kind of visual pun) on the family name, with babes standing on tuns. Around the canopy angels carry shields engraved with the arms of the families. To the east is a relief of the Last Judgement, the dead rising from their graves and angels playing trumpets over them. Some happy souls make it through the narrow entrance, but the majority receive the fire and brimstone treatment. A stone originally lay on top of the monument, but it was taken down in the 19th century as its great weight was a possible threat to its continued existence.

The most (in)famous member of the Babingtons was the young, rich and handsome Anthony Babington, born in Dethick, Derbyshire in 1561. Having grown up as a Catholic, he had been a page to Mary Queen of Scots. In 1586 John Ballard persuaded him to lead a plot to murder Queen Elizabeth I and rescue Mary from her imprisonment at Chartley near Stafford. Sir Francis Walsingham discovered the plot and that Mary wanted the death of Elizabeth. Babington ran away. Legend has it that he hid over the canopy in the church. He was arrested at Harrow and beheaded the same year, at the age of 25. Mary was executed the following year.

The church is normally open during daylight hours.

45. Lambley

Drinking the pubs dry

Grid Reference: 632452 (the post office in Main Street)

Directions: Take the Woodborough Road out of Nottingham. The village is signposted on the right after 3 to 4 miles.

"Dumble" is a localism referring to a dell with a stream running through it, in this case the Dover Beck. Several villages have their dumbles, but Lambley Dumbles became famous locally because of a custom attached to it – Cowslip Sunday – which has been compared to the tulip festival at Spalding.

Cowslip Sunday took place on the first Sunday of May, when the dumbles were full of picnickers and the streets were invaded by strangers. The Main Road was lined with refreshment stalls and the village children gained extra pocket money by selling bunches of cowslips they had picked from the fields. It was a big day for the working classes of Nottingham and the surrounding villages. On a fine day in the 19th or early 20th century it was not unknown for several thousand people to gather here, taking bunches of cowslips home with them to make wine.

The custom lasted from morning to evening and the visitors drank great amounts of alcohol in the village pubs, often causing them to run out of beer. Not surprisingly, violence often occurred: local newspapers of 1866 complained about the difficulty the police had to keep order. There was talk of finding another day for the festivities so as not to "desecrate the Sabbath", but somehow "Cowslip Saturday" never caught the popular imagination.

In a lament for Lambley's last windmill, one newspaper in the

The Main Street

1920s expressed surprise that the fairies still allowed cowslips to grow in the village. But it was precisely the shortage of cowslips that brought an end to Cowslip Sunday in the mid-20th century, when more and more land was being ploughed up.

No one knows when or why Cowslip Sunday began, although a local historian of the time suggested that it was a survival of May Day festivities. Lambley Dumbles still exist of course, and the area still attracts a small number of people on Cowslip Sunday. Sadly, they can no longer see vast expanses of cowslips.

46. Langar

Home of a rebel

Grid Reference: 723347

Directions: Langar is 12 miles south-east of Nottingham. Approaching the village from Cropwell Bishop, turn into Main Street and the rectory (now a private house) is at the end.

L angar Rectory dates from 1722 when the Reverend Bennett Sherrard, the grandson of Dr Robert Thoroton, was rector. It was built with some of the money Queen Anne bestowed on such properties. Langar's other famous son, Lord Howe, also agreed to supply some of the building materials in exchange for an area of land where the old parsonage had stood. Another rector who lived in the property was the Revd Edward Gregory, an astronomer with an observatory nearby.

Thomas Butler was the rector in 1834. His father was at the time the Bishop of Lichfield and Coventry. It was into this religious world that Thomas's son Samuel was born. Thomas expected Samuel to follow in his own and his grandfather's footsteps, but this was not to be. Samuel's doubts concerning ordination were extremely strong. He had suffered his father's tyranny at the rectory and was not prepared to take the cloth.

After some years in New Zealand, where he made a modest fortune sheep-rearing, Samuel returned to England to write a number of

The rectory, first home of Samuel Butler

books. Following his wishes, his final book to make the bookshops –
The Way of All Flesh – was withheld from publication until after his
death. The book is a thinly disguised autobiography containing a
highly critical account of his life at the rectory. It is set in Battersby-
on-the-Hill, with protagonists Theobald Pontifax (his father) and
Ernest Pontifax (himself). The book attacks the hypocrisies of religion
as Samuel saw them, and his family are viewed as philistines. The
book is considered one of the greatest works of the period: Sir Victor
Pritchett called it "one of the time-bombs of literature", and George
Bernard Shaw thought Butler one of the most important writers of the
19th century.

47. Laxton

Royal visitors to Laxton

Grid Reference: 720676

Directions: Laxton is 10 miles north of Southwell. Follow Hall Lane, opposite the church, to the remains of the castle.

Laxton is well known as the only village in Britain where the three-field system is still practised, but far less people know about its castle. The earthworks to the north of the village are a fine example of medieval castle remains, standing on land that is one of the highest areas in the county. The castle was probably built by John de Caux after the Norman Conquest. It lay in a fine position for the Royal Forest of Sherwood, of which the de Caux family were the keepers until 1287. This meant that they were responsible for the administration of the forest, ensuring that there was no poaching of its game. The castle was a motte and bailey structure (see Bothamsall) which would have

Some remains of the castle inner bailey

been made of wood and erected on the mound. A number of mon-
archs made use of the castle over its 300-year existence, whether just
passing through or on hunting expeditions. The castle was reached
through the two baileys, which as well as providing protection, also
contained the outbuildings and living premises of the servants.

The castle gradually decayed and became uninhabitable some-
time in the 14th century. About 200 years later the Roos family built a
manor house, complete with stables and brew-house, in the inner
bailey south of the castle remains. It was demolished in the late 17th
century, although the E-shaped layout can still be seen on the ground.
So, too, can some of the manor house's wood and stones that were salvaged for use in some of the village walls.

More information about Laxton is in a video shown at the visitors'
centre at the back of the Dovecote Inn.

48. Lenton

The pub prison

Grid Reference: 553389

Directions: Lenton is 2 miles west of the centre of Nottingham. The White
Hart is at the north side of Abbey Bridge and Gregory Street.

Two stone mounting blocks stand in front of the White Hart at Lenton, memories of the days before the car. The pub facade was
built in 1804 by landlord George Wombwell, but the building itself
dates from the 17th century when it was a farmhouse. It is said to be
built on the foundations of the Priory gate house. Between 1790 and
1804 the building was a coffee house, although at the back a small
two-storey brick building, with three windows per storey, was formerly a prison.

The Prison of the Court of Peveril may go back as far as William the
Conqueror. Lenton is at least the fourth place where the prisoners
were housed: first there was the Chapel of St James in Nottingham,
followed by Shire Hall and then Basford. The inmates were treated
very harshly in the early years.

The White Hart

From 1790 the landlord of the White Hart was also the jailer, and the prison continued until 1849 when the Court of Peveril ceased to function. Most later prisoners were said to have been debtors. The regime appears to have been quite informal by the time the prison reached the pub, the prisoners often acting as waiters, carrying out food and drink to customers on the bowling greens.

The White Hart was the focal point of a number of activities. The Lenton and Radford Society for the Prosecution of Felons met there, along with friendly societies. One of the earliest of these was the Amicable Society in 1797. The building has a number of bricked-up windows, a hangover from the infamous window tax of 1696 to 1851.

49. Littleborough

Toll Bar House

Grid Reference: 815831

Directions: Littleborough is 9 miles east of Retford. At Sturton le Steeple continue east along Church Street (Littleborough Road). The toll-house is at the junction with Thornhill Lane, 800 metres before the village.

For a village that now consists of only a church, five farms and a cottage (once the toll-house), it seems extraordinary that Littleborough used to be the Roman town of Segelocum. It was the most significant in the county not to stand on the Fosse Way. There was once a ford between Nottinghamshire and Lincolnshire which the Romans paved with cobble stones, thus providing access from Doncaster to Lincoln and York. Even today, when the water is low, these stones can still be seen.

The two-storey hexagonal building on the edge of the Lincolnshire border is a very rare survival in Nottinghamshire of a turnpike toll-house. It was built about 1825: the road from Littleborough Ferry to Clarborough (just outside Retford) was turnpiked under an 1824 act. The road was in bad repair but the levying of tolls made repair possible. The shape of the house was designed to enable the toll collector to see travellers coming from Coates, Cottam, Littleborough itself, North Leverton and Sturton-le-Steeple. The Ferry Boat Inn was in business in Littleborough until 1862 when a new road bypassing the village was constructed over the Trent. Standing on the river bank, the pub is a private house today.

The Proposed Table of Tolls for the Retford & Littleborough Road Bill – with the original punctuation unchanged – reads:

For every Horse or other beast, excepting an Ass, drawing any Coach, Barouche, Sociable, Berlin, Chariot, Landau, Chaise, Gig, Chair Phaeton, Caravan, Taxed cart, Hearse, Litter, or other suchlike Carriage the Sum of Ninepence.

Oxen or other cattle were charged at tenpence for every twenty, and calves, swine, hogs, sheep or lambs fivepence for the same number. The toll was doubled on Sundays. Exemptions applied to foot passengers, mail vehicles, military horses, vehicles carrying passengers to church or to vote, and animals going to water or pasture.

Turnpike tolls ended in different places at different times, but mainly between the 1860s and the 1880s with the passing of the Annual Continuance Acts. Littleborough toll-house closed in 1876 and the building was turned into a private house in 1965, with three rooms on the ground floor and three upstairs. A short row of the original outbuildings remains, consisting of toilet, coal shed and another shed of unknown purpose. Known locally as The Old Round House, the toll-house once also had a 2-metre high chimney.

The converted toll-house

50. Lyndhurst
A meeting place in the country

Grid Reference: 559579

Directions: Now a part of Mansfield, Lyndhurst is south-east of the town. To the east of the Mansfield Road (A60) just before entering the town, the Old Newark Road marks the southernmost point of any housing development. It is now a rough track, but the journey is not long. Less than 1 mile along the road, take the first turning right (the unmarked Black Scotch Lane). After 300 metres there is a farm on the right – it is probably sensible to park your car somewhere here as the terrain gets worse. Continue for 400 metres and you will then see the Forest Stone in a field on the left.

The former Moot Hall is a branch of the Yorkshire Bank today. In the centre of Mansfield, on the corner of the Market Place and Westgate, it bears the inscription "17HCHOM52". This signifies the date it was built, shown either side of the initials of the benefactor, Henrietta Cavendish Holles (Countess of) Oxford and Mortimer.

The countess had the stone – originally from the Market House on the site of the Moot Hall – moved to the site of the great forest court and swainmote. As the plaque on the stone says:

On this place the justice in Eyre met the great officers of the forest every seven years for the administration of its affairs, and here also the verderers met the swains or freeholders in a moot three times a year for the purpose of renting the pasture.

The Swainmote Dinner was held every Holyrood Day at the Eclipse in Mansfield until 1823, then at the Swan Hotel. The Old Mansfield Society revived the custom in the 1920s, and with the exception of the war years it continued until 1958.

The Forest Stone

51. Mansfield

Hot cross buns at Easter

Grid Reference: 535611

Directions: The Old Meeting House chapel is set back at the bottom of Stockwell Gate behind the old parsonage.

The Old Meeting House celebrates an intriguing custom every year. On Good Friday morning hot cross buns are given out from a table in front of the old parsonage. This is a practice that goes back to a bequest by Mary Mallatratt in 1894. She bequeathed £100, the interest from which was to be used to buy buns for Mansfield's poor children each Good Friday.

Mary was born into a local publican's family at Fulwood near Sutton-in-Ashfield on 24 September 1844. In the early 1870s she lived and worked in the Matlock area and married George Mallatratt

The Old Meeting House

in Matlock Parish Church. George was a successful and prosperous owner of the Blue Boar in Stockwell Gate.

Mary lost her only child while he was an infant. She then devoted her energies to aiding her husband at the Blue Boar and helping out at the Old Meeting House. This was one of the social centres of the town and Mary concerned herself with various social functions. A very business-minded individual, she continued managing the pub after the death of her husband on 28 December 1888. She died on 26 July 1891.

The only interruptions to the custom came during the wars. The busiest year was 1912, during a coal strike, when 2000 buns were given out. Some years ago an attempt was made to amalgamate the fund with other charities, but the temptation was resisted. The buns are still distributed in Stockwell Gate, or inside the Meeting House if it is raining. The pub was rebuilt shortly before George's death and now houses the Alliance and Leicester Building Society.

52. Mansfield

The deep grave

Grid Reference: 557598

Directions: Leave Mansfield via Ratcliffe Gate, Rock Hill and Southwell Road West. Turn right into Berry Hill Lane and park on the first road on the left. On the other side of Berry Hill Road, a few houses to the left, is a row of ancient upright stones. This is the entrance to Thompson's Field.

Thompson's Grave is in a stone-walled circle with several trees growing in it. A memorial stone marks where Charles Thompson, born 1714, was buried on 17 December 1784. He came from a wealthy family, and on the death of his mother in 1737 moved to London to seek work in the clothing industry. After proving his worth in the profession, the firm sent him to Persia on business. The shah unfortunately died during his stay, and in the troubles that ensued Thompson was forced to return to England.

In 1750 he became a partner in another firm and left the country again – this time for Portugal. He had the uncanny misfortune to be there in the great earthquake of 1755, which destroyed the house where he was living. He again managed to escape to England, but without either his money or the goods he had originally taken with him. This experience of the floods caused by the earthquake was to leave an indelible impression on him: he was horrified to see disinterred coffins floating on the water. His business partner advised him to return to Portugal to recover the lost goods and money. He returned again from Portugal a richer and a wiser man, deciding now to live on the interest of his £700 savings. Every day he took a walk to his favourite spot on the hill above Mansfield.

On his death, Thompson left £400 to the church to provide money for the poor and £600 to the educational charity established by Samuel Brunts, along with many other bequests. As he had previously bought his favourite piece of land, he had also arranged to be buried there, six metres under to ensure that his coffin would not stray. Hundreds of mourners watched the burial on a cold winter's day.

The site is on land belonging to the Brunts Charity. In the centre is a marble memorial plaque in a stone structure erected in 1932 by the Trustees of Brunts Charity in recognition of his philanthropic work.

The wall enclosing Thompson's Grave

53. Mapperley

The end of an era

Grid Reference: 587426

Directions: On the Woodborough road (B684) out of Nottingham, continue
for 2 miles. Turn right at the Mapperley pub into Porchester Road. The
hospital is on your right.

Nottingham's first psychiatric hospital was the General Lunatic
Asylum in Carlton Road in 1812. The increasing concern about
the need for such an institution was emphasised by the mental state
of George III. The asylum at Sneinton was, with the asylum at Bed-
ford, the first to be built following the County Asylums Act of 1808.
Dr John Storer was one of the main people responsible for its establishment. He wanted to run it on the same humanitarian principles as
the Retreat at York.

It was at first open to any patient from the county or borough,
whether they could afford to pay or not. In 1859, though, the Lunatic
Hospital – later known as Coppice Hospital – was built to accommodate fee-paying patients. Paupers remained at Sneinton.

As numbers at the general asylum grew, there was a recognised necessity to open another hospital for borough patients only, leaving
just the county patients at the Carlton Road site. George Thomas
Hine, the son of Thomas Chambers Hine (see Nottingham), won a
competition for the design of a new hospital. On Mapperley Hills, the
Nottingham Borough Lunatic Asylum – later known as Mapperley
Hospital – opened on 3 August 1880 with Dr Evan Powell as its medi-
cal superintendent. It was full almost as soon as it opened.

Here, care was taken to ensure that the patients were treated hu-
manely and great importance was given to gardening and sport. In
1924 electricity arrived at the hospital, and three years later the opening of the Majestic Cinema in Woodborough Road meant patients
were allowed to go there once a week.

From 1941 to 1966 Dr Duncan Macmillan was the physician superintendent at Mapperley. He is generally considered to have had a
radical approach to mental health care with his stress on community
care where possible, helping individuals in their own environment.

Mapperley Hospital from the west

Towards that end, Mapperley was the first psychiatric hospital in England* to open its doors in every ward in 1952. Railings were taken down and padded cells became store rooms in a movement away from institutionalisation. Aftercare was encouraged with the provision of a clinic, social workers and a day hospital. Later, many patients went to live in registered homes or special guest houses. International interest was aroused and many visitors in this field of medicine came to see how the idea worked. Mapperley Hospital was becoming increasingly redundant.

The closure of the hospital had been inevitable for some time, although it did not come until December 1994, which the local press labelled "the end of an era." The building is now called Duncan Macmillan House and some parts of the old hospital are now Health Care Trust offices.

---

* The first psychiatric hospital in the United Kingdom to open its doors was Dingleton Hospital, Melrose in 1949.

54. Mattersey Priory
The secluded priory

Grid Reference: 703895

Directions: Mattersey is 6 miles north of Retford. The way to the priory is signposted – it is at the end of Abbey Lane, a grassy path facing the Barley Mow Inn in the centre of the village. The track is 1 mile long and not necessarily of benefit to a car's suspension.

This is one of English Heritage's more obscure unmanned sights. Although in ruins, Mattersey Priory is the best preserved of the Gilbertine priories in England. Established by St Gilbert of Sempringham in south Lincolnshire in the middle of the 12th century, this is the only order to be founded in Britain. As such, it did not have to seek confirmation of policies from France or Italy. An uncommon feature is that the Gilbertine order accepted both sexes, worshipping in one place but living separately, and normally divided by a wall. In

The ruins of Mattersey Priory

this small monastery, though, there were only six regular canons (or-dained priests in a communal monastery). They were aided by 10 lay brethren, men who had taken a religious vow and worked the fields as agricultural labourers. There were hundreds of such small religious houses belonging to other orders in England in medieval times.

The priory was ideally situated for a religious retreat, close to woods filled with game and right against the River Idle with its plenti-ful salmon and perch. At the time of its foundation it stood on an is-land. In 1279 the priory was severely damaged by fire, much of the building and many records being lost. This badly strained the monas-tery's finances and was something from which Mattersey never fully recovered.

During the dissolution of the monasteries, the mother house at Sempringham went first in 1538, followed on 7 October by Mattersey itself, by which time there remained only a prior and four monks. Prior Thomas Norman was ordered to surrender the buildings to Henry VIII, for which he was given a pension of £22 13s 4d (£22.66) per annum. Although there is little left of the building, the layout can still clearly be seen – a small rectangular chapel and some accommo-dation buildings.

The priory is open during daylight hours.

55. Newark

Gopher remembered

Grid Reference: 799539

Directions: Newark is 17 miles north-east of Nottingham. St Mary's Church is at the side of Newark's Market Place.

Ringing the Gopher Bells is one of the traditions of Newark dating from the Middle Ages. It concerns a man named Gopher, a Dutch merchant (or Flemish engineer – sources are uncertain) who became lost in the fog in the Kelham area. He got stuck in the marshes and thought that all hope was lost until he started to pray. Then he heard

St Mary's Church, Newark

the sound of church bells at St Mary's in Newark and realised that he would be saved if he moved towards the sound.

On reaching Newark, Gopher decided to bequeath a sum of money for the bell-ringers of the town to ring at the same time in November every year, in order to help people caught in a similar predicament. The practice continues each year on the twelfth Sunday preceding Christmas. It continues each Sunday for six weeks in total, from 17.00 to 18.00 in place of Evensong. Unfortunately, it seems that the records of Gopher's gift have been lost.

56. Newark

The Beaumond Cross

Grid Reference: 800536

Directions: The Beaumond Cross is in the rest garden by the library, off London Road.

The Beaumond Cross is a tall, stone shaft with a statue at the base and various figures at the head. Although it is well preserved for a 14th century structure, the figures are too eroded for us to make any significance of them, and its origins remain a mystery. It once stood at the junction of Carter Gate, London Road, Lombard Street and Portland Street until increasing traffic through the town forced it to be moved to Beaumond Gardens, London Road in 1974.

Some have thought the cross is one of those King Edward I erected – at each place the funeral procession of his wife, Eleanor, stopped on its way to her burial in Westminster Abbey. The cortege was on its way from Harby in 1209, but the cross was constructed some time after this date and no sources have ever mentioned an Eleanor Cross in Newark.

Other sources have revealed that Beaumond was an area in Newark, just beyond the town boundary near here. The cross *may* have been a boundary marker, but the name Beaumond might also allude to the Beaumont family. If so, the cross could also be a monument to the Earl of Beaumont from Beaumont Leys in Leicester. He took the Bishop of Lincoln prisoner after King Stephen threatened to starve him if the bishop did not give up Newark Castle.

A religious association cannot be ruled out either because crossroads were associated with religious worship. A cross could also offer sanctuary to a threatened person. Whatever the origins of the Beaumond Cross, there will never be a shortage of speculation about its origin.

The enigmatic Beaumond Cross

57. Newark

Books to burn

Grid Reference: 799538

Directions: Byron's plaque is on the wall at the side of Porter's delicatessen in the Market Place.

S tories of Lord Byron – his many sexual conquests and support of the Greeks against the Turks – are well known. So, too, are his connections with Newstead Abbey and Southwell. Newark is rarely mentioned in relation to Byron, although the poet stayed at the Clinton Arms Hotel in the Market Place when his first book of poems was being printed. He financed it himself and the work was printed by Ridge – located on the opposite side of the Market Place to the hotel. A plaque marks the occasion.

Fugitive Pieces was published in November 1806 and was written when Byron was about 16. The poet had entered Cambridge Univer-

The Byron plaque

sity that year, and during vacations went back to Southwell where his mother lived. He was a well-known figure there and the reaction to his poems, particularly the erotic *To Mary*, was explosive. Tame by modern standards, the book inflamed the small town sensibilities of 19th century Southwell.

Byron's friend the Revd John Thomas Becher, under pressure from his father-in-law, was forced to urge Byron to destroy the copies. The poet promptly burned them and announced that he was working on another project that would be *"vastly* correct and miraculously chaste". The following year Ridge printed *Hours of Idleness* – a title of their choosing. It contained 30 poems, 19 of which had appeared in *Fugitive Pieces*. It was severely criticised by some reviewers, but helped to launch him as a poet.

The Newark Museum in Appletongate exhibits the original press which Ridge used for printing the two collections of poetry.

58. Newark

The neglected fort

Grid Reference: 791531

Directions: From the castle the Queen's Sconce is about 1 mile south. Walk along Castle Gate and Millgate. The entrance is through a recreation ground near the junction of Millgate, Boundary Road and Farndon Road.

Nottinghamshire marks both the beginning and the end of the Civil War between the Royalists and the Parliamentarians. It began with King Charles raising his standard – at Standard Hill in Nottingham on 22 August 1642 – and officially ended on 6 May 1646, the day after Charles's surrender to the Scots at the Saracen's Head (then called the King's Arms) in Southwell. There are many reminders of the war in the county, but perhaps none more impressive than the earthworks known as the Queen's Sconce (a Dutch word meaning "fort").

The sconce was built to defend royalist Newark from the attacking Parliamentarians. It was probably constructed after the second siege of Newark in 1644 and before the third and final siege beginning November 1645. The area covered is about 1 hectare, and the huge ramparts have four diamond-shaped corners where cannon protected the town from all angles. A vast array of storm poles protruded horizontally from the rampart wall. Surrounding the great ditch around the sconce was a palisade and beyond that were numerous pitfalls containing sharp spikes to deter the invaders. Makeshift accommodation for the soldiers would have been set up in the hollow of the fort.

Unfortunately, the Queen's Sconce is in a parlous state: the earthworks are being eroded by children playing on them and are generally being abused. There is at present no interpretation plaque and no indication to strangers of its historic importance. An action group has been formed, however, and it is hoped that something can be done to preserve this vital part of Newark's heritage.

The Queen's Sconce (south-east corner)

59. Nottingham
Death of a Chartist

Grid Reference: 566407

Directions: From the Waverley Street entrance of the arboretum, walk up the path between the lake and the aviary. Take the path on the right after the café and walk along it for about 150 metres.

The Feargus O'Connor statue

Feargus Edward O'Connor's statue in the arboretum raised a few eyebrows when it was first put there in 1859, four years after the MP's death. He was hated for his egotism and his erratic nature, but O'Connor was an idealistic, populist MP who represented his constituents well. For all O'Connor's faults, he was a remarkable and courageous man worth far more than a footnote in the history of English politics.

The Chartist movement began in 1836 with the drawing up of a charter by the London Working Men's Association. The charter called for six things: suffrage for every man over 21, a secret ballot, no property qualifications for MPs, payment for MPs, equal constituencies and annual parliaments. It was fiercely opposed to the Poor Law Amendment Act of 1834

which limited the poor's access to outdoor relief – to qualify for assistance they had to join a workhouse (see Upton).

From 1839 O'Connor was the firebrand leader of the Chartists. He
was an excellent orator and any speech he gave was bound to rouse its
listeners. He consequently gained great favour among the low-paid
framework knitters in Nottingham. By 1847 he was the only Chartist
MP ever elected and was congratulated by Marx and Engels. His
meetings in the Market Place attracted thousands of people.

In 1848, however – the year of revolutions in mainland Europe –
Britain was increasing in prosperity and Chartism was losing its
force. O'Connor presented the Chartist petition to the House of Commons but was ridiculed for faking a large number of the signatures.
Chartism was dead by 1850. O'Connor went mad two years later and
died in 1855. He was accused by many of causing the death of
Chartism, although 50 000 followed his funeral. Apart from the statue
in the arboretum, his tomb in Kensal Green Cemetery is the only other
public reminder of him that exists.

60. Nottingham

The poem that went on and on

Grid Reference: 574396

Directions: Bailey's plaque is on a building on the north corner of Fletcher
Gate and Middle Pavement.

The plaque on the wall announces that Philip James Bailey (1816-
1902) lived here. Born in Nottingham and educated at Glasgow
University, Bailey began writing his great poem *Festus* at his parental
home and birthplace at Basford between 1836 and 1839. His father,
Thomas Bailey, author of *Annals of Nottinghamshire*, described the
site in this way:

*On entering Basford station yard and passing through its tastefully
structured gatehouse, there may still be seen through the trees, which
border the small stream which separates the grounds from the station
yard a large, old-fashioned brick house.*

According to his father, Philip finished the first edition by the age of 20. The book was not published until three years later, though, when the anonymous work received considerable favourable attention – particularly in the United States – and went through a number of editions. It is essentially about the triumph of good over evil. Bailey wrote a number of other poems, but they were all incorporated into the same volume: he seemed incapable of writing more than one book. The result was that in 50 years Bailey had written an 800-page poem that was virtually unreadable – it was packed with dense type and subheadings in a low point size. This is perhaps the single factor which has prevented Bailey from achieving greater recognition. One of his verses is often quoted, however:

We live in deeds, not years; in thoughts not breaths;
In feeling, not in figures on a dial
We should count time by heart throbs; he most lives
Who thinks most, feels noblest, acts the best.

There is a bronze bust of Bailey by Albert Toft in front of the rear entrance to Nottingham Castle.

The Bailey plaque

61. Nottingham
The orchid king

Grid Reference: 577395

Directions: Trivett's tower is in Short Hill in the Lace Market. A good view of it is from outside the chancel of St Mary's Church, near the corner of Stoney Street and High Pavement.

L ouis Oram Trivett's old factory is a prominent structure with a courtyard called Trivett Square and the initials "LOT" inscribed over a doorway. Perhaps its most outstanding feature is a small tower which used to be the subject of some speculation: it was rumoured that Trivett, an important member of the Boy Scout Association, had it built so that he could watch the activities of scouts on the other side of the River Trent.

Trivett was a highly respected employer in the plain net lace industry and a local politician of long standing. The son of William Trivett, he was born in Mansfield on 26 August 1864 and educated at High Pavement School. He worked in the lace trade all his life. At 21 he was manager of the lace department of John Feilman and Co, and within six years he had his own business in Woolpack Lane. After a spell in Stoney Street, the firm finally settled in the premises in Short Hill.

The financial rise of Trivett is clear from his home addresses: starting off in the modest Noel Street, he moved to 4 Wilford Lane and then the impressive Grafton House in Loughborough Road, West Bridgford. He was a very public figure and was for many years county councillor for Ruddington, and then for West Bridgford following a change in county boundaries. For most of the time he was a Liberal-Unionist, only joining the Conservative Party towards the end of his life.

Trivett's great passion was the scout movement. He was a personal friend of the founder, Lord Baden-Powell, and honorary treasurer and secretary of the Boy Scout Association. He once presented a scout hut to the West Bridgford troop.

Trivett grew orchids and usually wore one in his buttonhole. On the arrival of the Philatelic Conference in 1927, he gave each of the

200 delegates one of the flowers. Friends nicknamed him the Orchid King. Trivett died in January 1933 and was buried in the Church Cemetery in Nottingham.

Trivett's tower

62. Nottingham
On the introduction of celery

Grid Reference: 570395

Directions: Newdigate House is on the north-west corner of Castle Gate and Maid Marian Way.

Newdigate House was built about 1675 and had a distinguished occupant between 1705 and 1711. Following the Battle of Blenheim in 1704, in which Marlborough's forces defeated the French, some French prisoners were sent on parole to live in England. Marshall Talland was one such prisoner. The conditions of his parole appear to have been lenient, though, and he was welcomed into the company of fellow aristocrats at Belvoir Castle and Melbourne Hall.

But Talland also had the common touch and fraternised with ordinary people. He is said, for example, to have taught Nottingham women how to make French bread and salads. He organised boxing and wrestling matches among the local boys. He discovered celery,

Newdigate House

hitherto unknown as a food in England, growing wild in Lenton marshes. The story is that he cultivated it in Newdigate House gardens, and in so doing helped introduce it to English kitchens.

Some of the stories surrounding Talland may be exaggerations, but it is clear that both the marshall and the town profited from his stay and that he wholeheartedly immersed himself in community life. He is even said to have sent a letter to Louis XIV in an attempt to discourage him from continuing the war.

The original house railings survive and are believed to have been built by Francis Foulgham, who lived in Nottingham from about 1710 until his death in 1749. Much later Newdigate House became the home of the United Services Club, and in the 1960s was severed from its neighbour by the appallingly destructive Maid Marian Way.

63. Nottingham
The redundant tunnel

Grid Reference: 565400

Directions: The entrance to the Park Tunnel is on the south corner of Upper College Street and The Ropewalk. An iron gate guards a series of steps, at the bottom of which you will find yourself in the tunnel itself.

Long-term residents of Nottingham are frequently surprised to learn of the existence of the Park Tunnel, particularly as it is so close to the heart of the city. Prominent city architect Thomas Chambers Hine became surveyor of the Newcastle Estates (with special reference to the Park) in 1854. Work had begun on the Park by other architects some time before. Hine was the mastermind behind the rapid transformation of the largely underdeveloped Park – once the Castle's backyard deer-hunting grounds – into a symmetrically laid out residential estate. The cutting of the tunnel was designed to provide a major entrance from Derby Road into the Park. Intended to allow passage for a carriage and six horses, the tunnel ranged from 10 metres wide at the Derby Road end to 15 metres at the Park end. It was 80 metres long with an impressive 16-step entrance – a spiral staircase – at the top of College Street.

The tunnel was a failure for two reasons. Hine had previously agreed with the owner, the Duke of Newcastle, that the gradient should not exceed one in 14, but it was one in 12. Added to this, by the time the tunnel was completed there were easier routes in and out of the Park. The grand tunnel was probably never used, and lapsed into obscurity.

The Park Tunnel near the centre of Nottingham

64. Nuncargate

The cricketer who made his own bats

Grid Reference: 502541

Directions: Follow Annesley Road from Hucknall. On the outskirts of Nuncargate turn left into Shoulder of Mutton Hill, then left again into Nuncargate Road a few metres further on. After Grainger Avenue, Chapel Street is the sixth turning on the left. Harold Larwood's house is number 17.

Cricketer Harold Larwood grew up in this house. He was born on 14 November 1904 and very soon became obsessed with the sport. As his family could not afford to buy him any cricket equipment he was forced to make his own bats. But at the beginning of his working life, a career in cricket was not an option. Like fellow cricketer Bill Voce, Larwood had to start working down the pit alongside the other working class men of the area.

Harold Larwood's house

But this did not deter the budding fast bowler. After being invited for a trial at Trent Bridge, it became evident that Larwood was a potential talent to be reckoned with. Nottinghamshire captain Arthur Carr tutored him, and Harold Larwood began a new career which was to take him from obscurity to international fame.

From 1925 to 1938 the former miner played in 21 tests for Nottinghamshire, although it was the test tour of Australia – the "body-line" tour – that caused so much controversy. "Body-line" referred to the ball being bowled directly at the batsman, usually forcing him to strike out. There would be six fielders positioned no more than 15 metres away to get a catch – the main form of wicket-taking with this type of bowling. It was the English captain, Douglas Jardine, who was responsible for encouraging this bowling method. Everyone thought the Australians invincible, but Larwood's bowling brought the Ashes back to England. Everyone, including rival captain Donald Bradman, had to admire Larwood's performance. Larwood was, nevertheless, later asked to apologise to the MCC for aggressive bowling, which he refused to do, and as a result never played again for England. "Body-line" bowling was outlawed by the MCC after the tour, although the following season Jardine presented Larwood with an ashtray marked "To Harold for the Ashes, 1932 to 1933. From a grateful skipper."

Larwood emigrated to the Australian sun with his wife and five daughters in 1949. He died in Sydney on 22 July 1995. Two plaques were erected in Nuncargate: one at his former home and the other at The Cricketers Arms, next to the field where he first played cricket as a young child. The Larwood and Voce pub in West Bridgford also commemorates the man and his opening bowling partner.

65. Old Clipstone

The King's lodge

Grid Reference: 604647

Directions: King John's Palace stands on private property. In Old Clipstone park near a side road – west of the main road – signposted "Warsop 3". Diagonally opposite this side road is a set of steps next to a bus shelter. At the top is a corrugated iron chapel and an excellent view of the ruins.

The name King John's Palace is a misnomer: it was in fact a hunting lodge and King John did not use it much. However, the ruin is a reminder of Nottinghamshire's royal past, of the days when Sherwood Forest occupied a much more extensive area. The lodge existed in 1164 and may have been built by Henry II. He enclosed it in an 8-mile park where deer roamed, and probably lived here for a time.

Until Henry IV a succession of kings used Clipstone. Richard I met William of Scotland here in 1194 on his return from capture by the emperor Henry VI. John used the lodge briefly on four occasions, and on the final occasion a huge amount of wine was drunk. Following a fire, a lot of building work was done in Clipstone under Henry III, but it is not known if he was ever a visitor. Edward I called a parliament to meet at the nearby Parliament Oak, and his son Edward II frequently came here.

King John's Palace

The decline started near the beginning of the reign of Henry IV, when the king gave the lodge to the Earl of March in recognition of his loyalty. The lodge was ruinous by 1525 and further damage was done to it during the Civil War. The surviving ruins probably date from Edward I.

66. Oxton

Old Ox

Grid Reference: 635532

Directions: Begin in Oxton village. Park near the Green Dragon, on the corner of Blind Lane and Windmill Hill. Old Ox is a little more than 1 mile up Windmill Lane and across the fields.

The hill fort of Old Ox (perhaps signifying "Old Works") is in the shape of an ellipse and almost certainly dates from the Celtic period. It is the best preserved one in the county. The ancient earthworks represent a camp with hills all around. There is also a ditch, up to a depth of 2 metres, all around the earthworks. The east side was made particularly steep for defence purposes, and entrance to the camp was from the raised path on the south side. The wooded area in the north had a particularly complex defence system.

The fort would later have served as a defence against the invasion of Emperor Claudius in AD43. The low-lying parts of England had conceded defeat within five years, although Nottinghamshire was a dividing line between the peaceful Corietavi (formerly called *Coretani*) tribe in flat Lincolnshire and the bellicose Brigantes in hilly Derbyshire. The latter continued fighting for decades. There is a smaller settlement immediately west of Combs Farm a mile to the north, where Roman pottery was found.

Old Ox viewed from the west

67. Papplewick
The pumping station

Grid Reference: 583521

Directions: The pumping station is 8 miles north of Nottingham. The appropriately-named Seven Mile House is in Mansfield Road (A60), exactly that distance from the centre of Nottingham. Turn right here into Burntstump Hill and then first left into Longdale Lane. Papplewick Pumping Station is on the left after 1 mile.

The population of Nottingham increased from 10 305 in 1739 to 50 220 in 1831, mainly due to the mechanisation of industry and a change in farming practice from crop raising to pasture. As the borough freemen would not allow the town to expand beyond its medieval limits, people were squashed into the same existing area. Disease understandably spread, one of the causes being contamination of the water supply by sewage and industrial waste. The River Leen during

The cooling pond with the engine house in the distance

this period – and later the River Trent – became inadequate to satisfy the demand for water.

A few water supply companies consequently formed, using steam engines to pump pure water from springs and wells. In 1845 the Nottingham Enclosure Act was passed, although it was 20 years before the main enclosure award came through. In the same year the water companies amalgamated to form the Nottingham Waterwork Company under Thomas Hawksley. In his time deep wells were sunk at the Park (1850), Sherwood (1857) and Bestwood (1871). Hawksley left when the company was taken over by the Corporation of Nottingham in 1890.

Corporation engineer Marriott Ogle Tarbotton was appointed in 1880 and saw a vital need to increase the levels of water production and storage. As a result Papplewick Pumping Station was built in 1884.* The jewel in the crown is the engine house. Ornately decorated and with stained glass windows, it contains two pumping engines that were among the last to be built by James Watt & Co. The station changed to electricity in 1922.

Papplewick Pumping Station ceased normal functioning in 1969, but was reopened in 1976 after being restored by a team of volunteers. It is open to the public and holds regular steam days.

Papplewick is open from Easter to the end of October on Sundays and Wednesdays from 14.00 to 17.00, and from November to Easter on Sundays from 14.00 to 16.00. Ring (0115) 963 2938 for details of steam days. There is an admission charge.

---

* Later, increasing water consumption led to the building of Boughton (pronounced "Booton" locally) Pumping Station in 1905 over an underground lake called Bunter Bed. At the time of writing (September 1997) the building is being restored.

68. Papplewick
Montagu's legs

Grid Reference: 546515

Directions: Follow Main Street (the B683) north through the village past the Griffin's Head, and Papplewick church is signposted on the left.

In 1795 Frederick Montagu of Papplewick Hall rebuilt Papplewick church, with the exception of the tower. His tomb, unusual because of its six legs, is in the churchyard. Montagu was a Commissioner of the Treasury at the time of the Fox-North coalition and a man with strong literary tastes. He put up a monument to Thomas Gray – a stone square with an urn on top – by the River Leen. He inscribed the following verse by Gray on it:

Beside some water's rushy brink
With me the Muse shall sit and think
At ease recline'd in rustic state
How vain the ardour of the Crowd
How low, how little are the Proud
How indignant the great.

A little further up the river, Montagu put up a similar memorial. This one was to the poet William Mason, friend and biographer of Gray. The inscription this time was taken from one of Mason's poems.

There are some coffin stones in the church depicting the professions of those buried there, including one in the porch wall with a symbol

Frederick Montagu's tomb

of a pair of bellows to represent an iron worker. Also of note is a tombstone marking the death of a Mary Farnsworth in 17012 (*sic*).

69. Pleasley Vale

Fires at the mills

Grid Reference: 516649 (Upper Mill)

Directions: Pleasley village is 4 miles from Mansfield and in Derbyshire, although Pleasley Mills are in Nottinghamshire. At the roundabout north of Pleasley, turn right into Common Lane (B6407) towards Shirebrook. After 200 metres turn right into Outgang Lane and then second right into the car park. Upper Mill is 800 metres further along Outgang Lane. Turn right down a footpath which will lead you to near the edge of the River Meden in Derbyshire. On the other bank is the Nottinghamshire mill. (There is a footpath from the car park along the south bank of the Meden, but the view is nothing like as picturesque.)

This wooded setting bears no signs of the original mill buildings, although the ornamental lake was once a mill dam. There have been a number of mills along the River Meden since the Middle Ages, but the cotton mill complex begun here in 1784 was the first such industry in the area. The business started as a partnership of five peo-

Upper Mill

ple: Henry Hollins, John Paulson, William Siddons, Thomas Oldknow and John Cowpe. Cowpe was only 25 years old and the only one to be salaried. The company underwent a number of name and management changes through the years, but it prospered and established a good reputation for high quality goods.

Following the original watermill, another was built some way downstream with a steam engine added in 1804. Both mills had to be rebuilt in the 1840s, however, after two separate incidents of fire. In 1859 there were 26 houses and a school for the workers' children. In 1893 600 people were employed at the site, by which time there was a railway passing alongside it. The name Viyella was then used for the firm's mixtures of cotton and wool. The name originated from Via Gellia in Derbyshire, where the firm owned another mill.

A third mill was built in 1913. This still exists, as do the other two mills that were rebuilt after the fire. Viyella House in Castle Boulevard dates from 1932 and was built by Frank Broadhead to house prestigious offices and warehouse.

70. Radford

Jack Johnson's horse

Grid Reference: 563408

Directions: Jack Johnson's house is at 87A Forest Road West, opposite Lawson Street.

U ntil the middle of the 19th century, 13 windmills stood in Forest Road, Nottingham. The house of one of the millers is all that exists today, but a story about him – probably apocryphal – has been passed down through the years.

Johnson owned a horse that was long past its best, and so decided to exchange it for a younger animal at Mansfield Market. On arriving there Johnson soon found a buyer for his horse, but had a lot of difficulty finding a replacement. He spent hours looking but still failed to find one that satisfied both his needs and his wallet. Throughout his search he made visits to a number of the surrounding hostelries. Towards the end of the day he finally found a horse which met his requirements. He was very proud of the creature and immediately rode it the 14 miles back to his home.

On waking the following morning, Johnson first went to see his precious new acquisition. He was shocked to find the same old horse he had sold the day before: in his drunkenness he had not noticed he had bought back his original horse, and for a considerable sum more than he had previously sold it. A few elementary cosmetic changes had been all that was necessary to deceive the befuddled miller.

The fact that similar stories were told of other local characters in other areas makes the truth of the story a little doubtful. The 19th century was a time when drink caused a great number of social and industrial problems, and this was possibly just a warning of the evils of drink, spread by one of the many temperance organisations of the day.

It could also be an example of the ridicule to which millers were then subjected – they were almost universally seen as heartless exploiters of the poor. The mere mention of the word "miller" at the beginning of a story would be enough to prepare listeners for a tale of contempt for the person they loved to hate.

The miller's house

71. Retford

Homes for sober elderly men

Grid Reference: 700812

Directions: Trinity Hospital is in Hospital Road, West Retford. From the Market Place, walk west along Bridge Gate and it is the first turning on the left.

Trinity Hospital is a product of the contents of the 17th century will of John Darrel, who was carrying out the wishes of his father as much as himself. John Darrel died in 1665 and bequeathed his home, West Retford Old Hall, as a hospital for 16 old men. His father once killed a man, and the bequest is thought to be a posthumous and belated atonement for this.

Under the provisions of Darrel's will, the building was to be known as the Hospice of the Holy and Undivided Trinity in West Retford, and to be managed by a board of governors with a "grave and ancient woman" as the nurse. The regime at the hospital was quite severe: expulsion from the hospital could have resulted from drunkenness, swearing, blasphemy and persistent failure to attend church. Prayers were read twice a day in the chapel. The men had to come from the Retford area, and they were then given 10 shillings (50p) per week, free coal and a new cloak every two years.

The hospital did not at first have a lot of money and it was not until 1794 that it had the full 16 men staying there. Money came in when the Chesterfield Canal Company bought a small patch of land, and also after the trustees shrewdly built Victoria Road, Darrel Road and Cobwell Road. They sold off the land at the side of them as building plots. West Retford, which was in 1847 referred to as a "miserable village", became transformed by the trustees. Many of the houses in this area have the inscription "T H" for Trinity Hospital.

By 1828 it became evident that the Old Hall would have to be rebuilt. Edward Blore,* the man who redesigned Lambeth Palace, completed this work in 1833. What we now see of the hospital is a lot

---

* Blore's connection with Nottinghamshire seems to be that he married the Vicar of Mattersey's daughter.

different from Blore's work, however. The building is in two clearly different styles because considerable additional work – notably the central part which includes the Audit Room – was done in 1872.

It is interesting to note that in 1873 one of the old men, Edward Beckett, began saving his beer allowance and three years later bought a stained glass window with the money. He pointed out to the other fifteen men that there was another window that could be treated in the same way if only *they* saved a little of their beer money, too. They were shamed into buying the other window – showing the Evangelists – the next year.

In spite of the rigours laid out in the will, Trinity Day was a bumper time for over-indulgence. Sometimes the celebration stretched to three days, with a great deal of rich food and drink supplied by the Cock Inn, Bridgegate. The hospital rules have been relaxed a little since the 17th century.

Trinity Hospital

72. Retford

A pile of scrap metal

Grid Reference: 705814

Directions: Appropriately, the cannon is in Cannon Square, opposite the parish church of St Swithuns.

The cannon in Cannon Square – the original site of Retford's medieval market – may now be one of the identifying items of the town, but it was nearly lost during World War II. It was historian Piercy's idea to have the cannon in Retford as he was the proud father of a brave soldier who had fought at the Battle of Alma in 1854. Corporal Charles Piercy, aged 21, is noted for his vivid descriptive accounts of the war. The weapon, weighing more than 1000 kilograms and dating from the year after Alma, was thus brought to the town as a celebration of the victory over the Russians in the Crimean War. It was paid for by prominent local citizens and arrived by rail in April 1858. For a

The cannon in the square

year no one could agree on where to place the "Earl of Aberdeen", which was nicknamed after George Hamilton Gordon, the Prime Minister from 1852 to 1855.

Cannon Square is now a quiet place, but over the years many events have taken place here. Cheeses used to be sold in bulk around the cannon at fair times, and F. Colton, the town crier and mace-bearer, used to announce important occasions from the church gates a few paces away.

An end very nearly came to the cannon in 1942. Retford's Street Salvage Stewards instructed the town council to collect the railings in the square, as well as the gun, to be melted down as scrap metal in the war effort. The cannon was consequently taken away but bought and hidden by a town solicitor. In 1949 the cannon re-emerged and was set back in its usual place.

73. Retford
The house by the air raid shelter

Grid Reference: 706811

Directions: From the Market Place, Grove Street is off to the east and Amcott House is on the right.

Amcott House was the 18th century home of the Whartons, a family of woollen drapers. It is on the site of a 17th century house that belonged to the same family. Sir Wharton Amcotts was MP for the Borough of East Retford and probably designed the present building as a town house in the 1770s. There is a large garden at the back and originally there was a garden at the front as well.

It was home to the Peglers, the owners of the Northern Rubber Company, from the 1870s. Until 1986, when the house was turned into a museum, it was the offices of Bassetlaw District Council. Now it contains some personal items that belonged to the Peglers, and a sign marked "Shambles" in relief which was taken from an area of butchers' shops in the town in 1980. There are also splendid ornamental ceilings and a wrought iron staircase. At the front of the house is the Tourist Information Centre which is housed in a former World War II air raid shelter.

Amcott House

There is a memorial tablet dedicated to Sir Wharton Amcotts in the chancel of the parish church of St Swithuns:

To the memory of Sir Wharton Amcotts of Kettlethorpe Park, in the County of Lincoln, baronet, who represented the respectable borough in Parliament during 20 years.

Amcotts died on 26 September 1807, aged 67.

74. Rufford
Savile's Broad Ride

Grid Reference: 645655

Directions: Rufford Country Park is 13 miles north of Nottingham. It is east of the Old Rufford Road (A614T).

Gilbert de Gant, the Earl of Lincoln, founded Rufford Abbey about 1148 for a group of Cistercian monks. On dissolution in the 1530s, Henry VIII gave the property to George Talbot, the fourth Earl of Shrewsbury. The sixth Earl of Shrewsbury turned the abbey into a country house which passed the following century to the Savile family, who owned it for over three centuries (1626 to 1938).

Sir George Savile was the seventh baronet and did a great deal to improve the property. Savile wanted to be in the vanguard of fashion, and with this in mind he built a bath house and garden pavilion in 1729. Bath houses were rare at the time, and this one had two towers and a portico with a balustrade round the roof. The water supply was from a nearby dyke and passed through an ornamental canal also built by Savile. The bath house was turned into an orangery-cum-winter garden in 1889. It was renovated in 1995.

Another of Savile's designs, influenced by the extravagance of Versailles, was the Broad Ride. This wide grassy path leads from the car park near the mill down to the remains of the abbey. The beech trees that once lined it were removed in World War II.

Rufford is now a country park open daily until dusk. Admission is free, although there is a parking charge at weekends, on bank holidays and during the school summer holidays.

The Broad Ride

75. Saundby

The bell-frame museum in the church

Grid Reference: 785879

Directions: Hall Farm is in the village, east of Saundby Road. Walk through it to find the church at the back on the right.

The visitor to the redundant church at Saundby is greeted by a collection of three bell-frames in the north aisle. The history of this mini-museum dates back to the mid-1970s when a donor in Rempstone village offered to have the church bells restored. They had long since ceased to ring, and the Southwell Diocesan Guild of Church Bell-Ringers began by taking the bells out and removing the old frame. They discovered that the frame (built 1722 to 1723) was an early example of work by Nottingham bell-founder Thomas Hedderly; it is one of perhaps only three of his remaining today. The bell-ringers then got permission from the parish to preserve the frame, but for some years it lay in the garage of the museum founder, George Dawson.

Eventually the Redundant Churches Fund (now the Churches Conservation Trust) found a place at Milton Mausoleum. While the RCF carried out repairs at Milton, however, the frame had to be moved, which is when it was transferred to its permanent home at Saundby. Saundby Church has been redundant since the end of the 1970s and had previously had its bells taken out due to fear of theft. They had been stored at St Mary's in Nottingham, but were subsequently brought here at the same time as the Rempstone bell-frame.

The church acquired its next frame in 1984. This other long-term non-ringer came from Kinoulton and is an interesting piece made by bell-founder Edward Arnold of Leicester in 1794. There are a number of surviving frames of his, and although this is in good condition and was originally thought reusable, this was not to be.

The third bell-frame (built in 1756) came from Morton-cum-Fiskerton in 1990. It was in a very bad state, and when the bells were to be rehung it was not capable of taking their weight. It is a very unusual frame for only two bells and is of the short-headed kind – the other two being of the big grillage type. Only two others of this type are known to survive in the county. This minnow is sandwiched between its two big brothers in the church.

The "museum" was never an intentional idea, but something which simply sprang up as a result of a series of circumstances. Disused bell-frames are usually preserved *in situ* – as at Gringley on the Hill – and the bell normally rehung lower down the tower. There was no room for these three frames in their original situations, but since they were considered important enough to be worth preserving, they were mercifully saved from being used as firewood.The little bell-frame museum at Saundby is unique. Some other churches, such as All Saints at Theddlethorpe in Lincolnshire, have isolated disused bell-frames on display, but this is the only church to have a collection of them.

The Guild puts bell-frames it does not preserve to interesting fund-raising use. The good wood is used to create souvenir items such as key fobs, and frames from Papplewick in Nottinghamshire and Stathern in Leicestershire have been used for this purpose.

Although Saundby Church is kept locked, there is a notice in the porch explaining where to obtain the key.

The old bell-frame from Morton-cum-Fiskerton

76. Scarrington

Temporary home for stray animals

Grid Reference: 735415

Directions: The pinfold is clearly visible next to the famous pile of horseshoes. This is in Mill Lane, opposite the church.

Pinfolds were often situated in or near the centre of a village. They date from medieval times when the open-field farming system was practised – a time when stray animals were common. A pinder would round them up and keep them in a pound until the owner paid a small fine. The pinder's wages here came in part from the farmers and cottagers. In 1789 they paid 2d – less than 1p – and 10d per annum respectively. The bulk of his money was from the fines collected, such as 1d for a horse, 4d for a pig and 2d for 20 sheep. The present pinfold here was built in the mid-19th century to replace a much older one. It was repaired in 1989.

At over 2 metres high, Scarrington is one of the tallest pinfolds in the county. It is also circular like those at Flintham, Low Marnham, Norwell, Screveton and Syerston. Pinfolds died out with the coming of enclosures.

Scarrington pinfold

77. Scrooby

The home of archbishops

Grid Reference: 654909

Directions: Scrooby is 2 miles south of Bawtry. Scrooby Manor House is the last house in Manor Road, but it is a private residence and best viewed from the distance of the adjacent Station Road.

The site of Scrooby Manor House has a recorded history going back to 1207. King John stayed here in 1212. Some have referred to the previous building as the palace or the house of the Archbishops of York because a number of them are known to have stayed here and entertained royal guests. In 1503 Princess Margaret Tudor spent the night here after Babworth (*q.v.*) on her way to Edinburgh, and Cardinal Wolsey stayed here for a month in 1530, just two months before his death. In 1541 Henry VIII held a Privy Council here.

The Manor House is probably most noted for its connection with

Scrooby Manor House

the Brewster family. In 1575, when the property is said to have been a bit run down, William Brewster senior was responsible for the administration of the estate. He later became postmaster on this major route to the north, and his son took his place shortly after his death in 1590. William Brewster junior came under the influence of Robert "Troublechurch" Browne's preaching, and between 1606 and 1607 Scrooby Manor House was the meeting place for the Separatist Church. Other future leading Pilgrim Fathers such as Richard Clyfton of Babworth, John Robinson of Sturton le Steeple and the young William Bradford from Austerfeld attended. This was the second Separatist Church after the one established in the Old Hall at Gainsborough.

Charles I demolished the house in 1636 or 1637, although parts of it are incorporated into the existing structure which was built as a farmhouse about 1750. In 1910 Everard L. Guilford, in his book *Nottinghamshire*, wrote that Scrooby lived by its American visitors. At the time this was one of their main visiting places and Guilford noted that the "picture postcard merchant does a roaring trade." Entrance to the house was 1 shilling (5p), but the public are no longer admitted. The village today is much more peaceful.

78. Selston

A Norman ruin

Grid Reference: 462513

Directions: Wansley Hall is 10 miles north-west of Nottingham and 2 miles south of Selston. On the south side of Wansley Lane, it is near the crossroads with Flatts Lane, Main Road and Wilhallow Lane.

The de Wandeslies lived in or around this area when the Domesday Book was compiled in 1086, although there is no evidence of their former manor house. The existing roofless ruin dates from the late Norman period – about 1200 – and would have served as the family's rather modest home. As the administrative hub of a farming community, there would have been a number of associated buildings

Wansley Hall from the north

around here. It is thought that there are remains of these buildings below ground, although above there is only a barn.

After a number of changes of ownership, the hall passed to Arthur
Skevington in the 1970s. It had by then been uninhabitable for over
10 years, the roof having partially fallen in in 1960. The estate was
sold after the death of Skevington in 1987.

The north part is the old hall proper – the south section having
been added far later – and in size (7.5 metres by 13 metres) it is com-
parable with other manor houses of its kind, the most obvious, perhaps, being Boothby Pagnall in Lincolnshire. The interior shows no
original features and is a mixture of different centuries.

79. Skegby

Beaten for her beliefs

Grid Reference: 493609

Directions: Skegby is 2 miles north of Sutton-in-Ashfield. The Quaker House is in the village, in Mansfield Road. A little east of the church, the private house is set back 20 metres.

Elizabeth Hooton lived in Skegby and may have spent some years in the Quaker House.* She is an important figure in the county and deserves more recognition. In the early 1640s, before the establishment of the Society of Friends, Hooton rebelled against formal religion – almost at the expense of her marriage. Her husband, Oliver, was at first reluctant to share his wife's ideas on the conventions of the established church, the ministry and the church order, but eventually came round in part to Elizabeth's views.

Elizabeth was at first a Baptist, but soon grew discontented and held secret meetings at her husband's farmhouse. At the time, the young George Fox was forming ideas which would soon evolve into the Quaker movement. Fox described Elizabeth as a "very tender woman" and his life has a parallel with hers in that he spent a lot of time harassing the clergy and being persecuted and imprisoned for his beliefs.

Society in the 17th century was dominated by men; women were regarded as second-class citizens. Quakerism was revolutionary in that it saw no distinction between the sexes. In this context it is at least understandable why there should have been such animosity towards Elizabeth Hooton. She was first sent to prison in Derby for reproving a priest in 1651, and the next year jailed in York Castle for similar offences in Rotherham. The sights she saw there disgusted her. As the wife of a reasonably wealthy farmer, prison was an eye-opener, and Elizabeth strove to improve conditions.

After Oliver's death in 1661, Elizabeth left to visit the United States at the age of 60. She had some difficulty finding a passage because ships' captains risked a £100 fine for transporting Quakers. On

---

* Near the village was a graveyard where Quakers were buried.

The Quaker House

finally landing in the country, she was imprisoned in Boston. The Governor, John Jackson, was extremely antipathetic to those he considered witches, and Elizabeth began a long round of further imprisonment and violent treatment at the hands of her religious persecutors. At one point she was left to starve in a forest, but managed to find her way out to Rhode Island and eventually England.

Some time after Elizabeth's return to England as an itinerant preacher, she left for the West Indies with George Fox and a group of other Quakers. Following a visit to Barbados, the company then went to Jamaica, which is where Elizabeth died and was buried in 1672. In her time she not only waved the flag of Quakerism and women's independence, but also carried weight as a prison reformer some years before Elizabeth Fry.

80. Sneinton

Cave dwellers

Grid Reference: 584395

Directions: Sneinton Hermitage is the name of the road as well as the cave. It is 200 metres from Manvers Street, on the north side of the road, opposite Windmill Court. A plaque records the restoration of the cave, which can clearly be seen in spite of a gate barring the entrance.

Nottingham is well known to be honeycombed with caves, although there are few accounts of people living in them. The largest set of caves was at Sneinton, just a little to the east of the city, and what stories there are of the cave dwellers make fascinating reading.

Sneinton Hermitage is the site where caves still exist, but is nothing now compared to the number that existed in the 19th century. There were over 300 metres of sandstone cliff with cave houses hollowed out all along. Such houses are known to have existed in the 16th century, but most went at the end of the 19th century and the beginning of the 20th. They had different rooms with windows, doors and chimneys. Near the surviving caves there were two pubs by the cliff face – the Earl Manvers and the White Swan.

There was an account in the *Weekly Express* by a Miss Bolderston who, at 85 years of age, lived in one of the almshouses on Park Street. She used to live in a house on top of the rock dwellings and had vivid recollections of her youth. On 10 May 1829 the Earl Manvers was destroyed by a fall of rock. Mrs Flinders lived in one of the rock houses at the time and her sons had arranged to take her to Barton Wake by boat. They had to pull her from her bed as her home collapsed. The landlady of the pub was unhurt, although half of the room where she was sleeping was demolished.

Many of the cave houses were cleared on the coming of the railways which cut into the west face of the cliff. Along with them went a way of life. There was a big cavern down 52 steps where young people held amateur theatricals and concerts, and at the bottom of Lees Hill was a well which provided water for the inhabitants of the caves. A man called Tansley kept his horse in one of the caves. Another pub, the White Swan, had a brew-house and outbuildings, and on one occasion half a ton of soil burst through landlord Sam Eyres's roof.

Rock houses stood all along the east side, from the present Lees Hill Footpath to the now derelict police station. In one was a man called Beecroft who was thought to be a Luddite. A story claims that in order to obtain sand to sell he tunnelled into the rock until he had to be stopped for fear that he would undermine St Stephen's Church. People also said that a madman was chained to a wall at the back of Beecroft's house. The rock dwellers had ceased to live in the caves for some 40 years when the road was widened and the western caves met the same fate as the others.

Sneinton Hermitage

81. Southwell

Cranfield House

Grid Reference: 703539

Directions: Southwell is 12 miles north-east of Nottingham. From the Saracen's Head in the centre of the town, turn into Church Street. There is a free car park on your first left. Cranfield House is the third house down from the car park entrance, almost opposite Southwell Minster Chapter House.

Cranfield House is a Queen Anne building of about 1709. It was originally called Oxton I and was one of a number of prebendal houses here. An earlier Oxton I was set back some distance from the road and was ruinous by the 1690s. Cranfield House was built even further back on the same land. It represented the height of fashion

Cranfield House

and was built by George Mompesson shortly after the death of his father in 1708.

From 1688 George was the prebendary of Oxton I. His father was
William Mompesson, the famous hero of Eyam in Derbyshire and
holder of the prebend of Normanton. George was the only beneficiary
of what was left of William's estate after he had some years previously
given a large part of his property to his offspring. The designer of
Cranfield is unknown, although a number of people have commented
on the similarity between this and Mompesson House in Salisbury,
built in 1701 by Charles Mompesson. When George died in the early
1730s he was a wealthy man.

The remaining prebendal houses are laid out to the west of the
minster on Westgate, and north and east of it in Church Street. In
clockwise order they are: Dunham, Rampton and Sacrista (Westgate),
and Norwell Overhall, North Muskham, Oxton I, Woodborough, Normanton and South Muskham (Church Street). According to Pevsner,
Cranfield is the best designed of them all.

82. Southwell

The Southwell Pence

Grid Reference: 702538

Directions: The minster is in the centre of the town.

S outhwell Minster marks the end of a journey on foot from Nottingham which is known as the Southwell Gate. The custom was revived in 1980, after many years. It originally started in 1109 and
probably ended at the time of the dissolution of the monasteries in the
late 1530s. Thomas of Beverley asked Nottinghamshire parishes to
contribute towards a new mother church at Southwell. An annual
Whitsuntide procession thus began, starting from Nottingham and
led by the mayor, the town dignitaries, members of the clergy and the
general public.

Southwell Minster

On the way there would be dances by morris men who would drink freely at the various hostelries en route, generating a festive atmosphere. Pony and donkey races took place at Southwell. The only surviving vestige of this is the races near Rolleston. It was traditional for the Southwell Pence to be taken to the north porch of the church.

The revived custom begins at the Market Square in the centre of Nottingham with morris men dancing a display before the Council House. The mayor then gives the Southwell Pence – a silver mark equivalent to 67 pence – and the procession leaves the square. They pass via Wheeler Gate and Middle Pavement to Hermitage Square in Sneinton where there is a brief dance, and then along the Southwell road (A612) to arrive for a service at the minster at 18.30. Money is collected on the way for charities.

83. Southwell

When the treadmill turned

Grid Reference: 704543

Directions: From the Saracen's Head in the centre of the town, walk north-east into King Street. Continue into the Burgage and the House of Correction is down a little road near the police station.

The House of Correction which today is in ruins on Burgage Green was not the first prison here – that house was built in 1611 and underwent multiple repairs. What exists today is the gatehouse of a later prison with bars and grids. It was built in 1807 by Richard Ingleman, who later built the Assembly Rooms in 1810 and the Old Grammar School in 1819.

This prison was larger than the previous one and more care was taken with security. The number of inmates increased more than fivefold on its opening. This was intended to house prisoners from the

The House of Correction

county, although it was not a place for dangerous criminals, more for misfits and paupers. Throughout the years additions were made: new wards, a governor's house and, more significantly, a six-storey prison block. The whole premises were enclosed by a boundary wall.

The regime was harsh: the prisoners rose at six in the morning, worked for more than 12 hours and had to turn the lights out at six in the evening. In spite of the slight nature of their crimes, security had become a great issue because fewer people were now transported overseas or hanged. It was thought that criminal tendencies could be cured by hard work. To this end, treadmills were later introduced in the belief that they would tire and demoralise the prisoners. There does not appear to have been any practical use for them in this prison, such as harnessing them for work. Prisoners working these tread-mills, however, received "wheelpence" of a penny a day.

A new enlightenment towards prisoners gradually permeated Victorian society and the old-fashioned House of Correction was closed in 1880. Although there is only one storey left, one of the walls from the prison block remains, the windows bricked up. A lot of the boundary wall is also present, visible particularly from the Lower Kirklington Road. The remains became a lace factory first of all, although a great fire caused tremendous destruction in 1973.

84. Stapleford

Homes for knitters

Grid Reference: 495374

Directions: Travelling east from the centre of Stapleford on the Nottingham road, the cottages are on the right, opposite West Avenue. The house numbers are 106 to 112.

The four lacemakers' and lace menders' cottages in Nottingham Road date from the beginning of the 18th century and are a throwback to the days when lacemaking was a prominent occupation in the area. The domestic dwellings themselves are two storeys high with a top storey having more spacious windows both at the front and the back to permit maximum daylight. They are typical of houses of their kind.

The story of William Lee's invention of the stocking frame, which formed the basis for later adaptations for producing machine-made lace, is perhaps well-known, but nonetheless deserves a mention. Lee was born in 1564 or thereabouts, but it was not until the 20th century that his achievement was officially recognised. He was educated at Cambridge – thought to have been Christ's and St John's – where he gained an MA. It is not certain if he was ever a clergyman, and there have been improbable romantic notions of his eagerly watching his girlfriend or wife hand knitting, hoping somehow he could perfect a device to give him more time with her. More prosaically, he could have simply been profit-motivated. Possibly, on the other hand, he wanted to ease the conditions of lace workers in general, although on balance this seems a bit doubtful.

Whatever the motive, the stocking frame was invented in 1589 and Lee tried to get Elizabeth I to give him a patent. When she refused, he emigrated to France with the frame, and although Henry IV was inter-

Four lacemakers' cottages

ested, he was killed in 1610. It is unknown when Lee died, but it has been suggested that he died of a broken heart and in penury. Lee's brother brought the frame back after his death.

Thomas Hammond, in 1768, is thought to have been the first to adapt a stocking frame for producing lace. But the lace boom of the early 19th century was really begun by John Heathcoat, whose invention in 1808 twisted the threads instead of looping them. Lee's stocking frame was, nevertheless, the basis of the modern stocking machine used today.

There are similar houses, although of a slightly later date, at 118 to 122 and 119 to 121 Nottingham Road.

85. Staythorpe

Homes for workers

Grid Reference: 752536

Directions: Staythorpe is 5 miles from Newark. The cottages are in Staythorpe Road, south-east of the hamlet and close to the level crossing.

Thomas Cecil Howitt was a 20th century architect most noted for his considerable contribution to the cityscape of Nottingham, particularly in the 1920s and 1930s. The Howitt Partnership built the cottages at Staythorpe. By the early 1950s, Howitt was limiting the time he spent at his architectural practice because he wanted to concentrate on RIBA business, but his style is, nevertheless, still very prominent here. The group began work on Staythorpe Power Station "A" in 1946 and the station started working in 1950.* The 13 cottages were originally designed to house the power workers, in so doing vastly increasing the population of the tiny hamlet.

Howitt was born in Hucknall to parents from Lancashire. He attended Nottingham High School until he was 15 and then began an

---

* The larger station "B" was built in 1956, although not officially opened until 1962.

apprenticeship under the noted architect Albert Nelson Bromley. After a short architectural education in London, Howitt came back to Bromley's office in Nottingham until 1913. After World War II he joined the Nottingham City Engineer's Department to build "homes fit for heroes".

Howitt built the Sherwood estate council houses and was also responsible for Wollaton Park estate which was constructed from land bought from Lord Middleton in 1924. Before establishing his own business, Howitt had built 6000 domestic dwellings and a new Council House for the city. In his own practice he went on to build many of the city's landmarks, of which these are just a few examples: Raleigh Head Offices in Radford Boulevard; Martin's Bank (now O'Neill's) in Upper Parliament Street; the Woolwich Equitable Building Society Offices in Old Market Square; and the YMCA in Shakespeare Street. Howitt moved to Orston in Nottinghamshire in 1961 and died in September 1968.

The power workers' houses

86. Strelley
Holes in the ground

Grid Reference: 514419 (near the Broad Oak pub)

Directions: There are some bell pits adjacent to the Broad Oak, some to the west of Bilborough Road and others on either side of the road leading to Strelley.

The coal industry in the East Midlands is now in terminal decline, but it was an important industry in the area for hundreds of years – the Willoughby and Strelley families were involved in mining from the 16th century. Wollaton Hall stands as a magnificent memorial built on the financial foundations of the black diamond, but evidence of coal extraction itself is scanty. This is why the early bell pit remains in the fields between Strelley and Bilborough are so interesting.

Diagram of a bell pit

Opencast is the earliest and most primitive form of mining, when the soil and subsoil are removed to reveal underneath the coal to be extracted. The next method of obtaining the coal was by creating bell pits, involving the sinking of small holes or shafts down to where the coal deposit lay relatively near the surface, to a depth of perhaps 6 metres. It was uneconomical to sink a deeper pit. Coal was then dug around the bottom and sides of the pit so that a cavity was formed in the rough shape of a bell. Work was continued there until the sides of the pit seemed in danger of caving in. The pit was then abandoned and another one started nearby. The coal was carried up to the top in baskets on a rope.

The bell pit remains at Strelley are perhaps from the 17th century. A number of circular mounds betray pit workings – the spoil accumulated around the pit to create a rim, and although an exhausted pit was usually filled in by pushing the spoil back, hollows are still in evidence. They vary greatly – some might show a slightly raised surface, whereas others may have a rim more than 1 metre high, the pits often being the same depth. Also in the fields are the remains of the primitive old track that was used, probably in the 18th century, to transport the coal to a road from where it would be carted to town. The coming of the canals provided a cheap alternative mode of transport.

87. Sutton-in-Ashfield
Celebrations at the viaduct

Grid Reference: 520598

Directions: Take the Sutton road out of Mansfield. King's Mill Lane is on the left immediately after a petrol station. Park at the end of the road and walk at the side of the reservoir for 30 metres. The viaduct is on the left.

One of the things Mansfield is noted for is the viaduct spanning the town. Less known is the five-arch King's Mill Viaduct on the outskirts which once carried the Mansfield to Pinxton pre-locomotives and was the scene of great celebrations on its opening.

Engineer Jessop originally intended to extend the canal at Pinxton to Mansfield. However, the contours of the land made this impossible, so plans for the railway were drawn up in 1811. It took years for Parliament to grant permission, but the railway was eventually opened on Easter Tuesday in 1819. It caused tremendous excitement in the area: people travelled from miles around to see the first loads of coal arrive in Mansfield. The financial advantages to the town were obvious – the price of a ton of coal plummeted from 12 shillings (60 pence) to eight shillings and sixpence (42.5p).

The owners of the railway and their friends met at the Swan Inn in the town and left on horseback to ride up the Alfreton road to the viaduct 1.5 miles away. They were joined by hundreds of people on foot and at the viaduct about 1000 people congregated, lining the road and spilling out into the fields. In Mansfield bells rang out all day to maintain the electric atmosphere. Ten wagons of coal had come from Pinxton colliery and workmen stood on them waving laurel branches. When the men arrived in Mansfield they were treated to pub dinners. The coals were released into the market place. They were lit and continued to burn into the night.

At the start of the railway track at Pinxton Basin the wagons were pulled by bullocks and horses to Kirkby. At the top of the hill they then had a downward path to Mansfield, the curves in the tracks serving as brakes. On the return journeys stone was loaded on the wagons to transport to the canal, and it was a source of local pride that this was used to rebuild the Houses of Parliament after a fire in 1833. The only objectors to the railway, not unnaturally, were stagecoach owners and wagoners. The locomotive era came to an end in 1847 when the Midland Railway Company bought the line, and King's Mill Viaduct fell into disuse in 1849.

The logo "1817 M & P" can still be seen on the bridge, serving as a reminder of the horse-drawn railway.

King's Mill Viaduct

88. Swingate
The ugly duckling

Grid Reference: 497438

Directions: From the war memorial in the centre of town, turn by Sainbury's into the High Street. Continue over the motorway and turn right along Swingate by the pub. On the right before the end of the street is Babbington Road. Turn into it and the tower is straight ahead.

A relatively new addition to the area's heritage, Swingate water tower was completed on 11 July 1950. The original water source had been near the Holy Well in the Watnall region (*q.v.*), although a leak led to the call for a better source. At the start of its existence the concrete tower was considered incongruous, but now it has become a treasured landmark by locals.

Kimberley Town Council, in conjunction with Broxtowe Borough Council, has tried to get Severn-Trent Water to light up the building at night as with Kimberley mortuary chapel (*q.v.*), but the attempts have been unsuccessful.

Swingate Water Tower

89. Thieves Wood
Whitaker's birds

Grid Reference: 544569

Directions: Thieves Wood is 12 miles north of Nottingham on the Mansfield road (A60). Before entering Mansfield, take the Kirkby road shortly after Newstead Abbey. After 500 metres turn right into the B6139 and park in the second car park – on the left. Opposite the car park is a path. A little more than 1 mile along this, the Bird Stone is at a junction on the left.

The Bird Stone in Thieves Wood is a replacement of the original. The former Bird Stone read:

This stone was placed here by J Whitaker of Rainworth Lodge, to mark the spot where the first British specimen of an Egyptian nightjar was spotted by A Spinks on 23 June 1883. It is only the second occurrence of the bird in Europe.

Albert Spinks was a gamekeeper who lived opposite the Bessie Sheppard Stone on the edge of Harlow Wood. He had been firing at a rabbit and the sound caused the bird to fly out so Spinks shot it. It was only by chance that he mentioned this to the naturalist Whitaker before disposing of it. The very grateful Whitaker salvaged the bird and had it stuffed.

Joseph Whitaker was the elder son of Joseph Whitaker of Ramsdale, where the younger man was born. He was educated at Uppingham School and inherited a love of the outdoors from his father, who was one of Bendigo's backers. Whitaker lived most of his life

The Bird Stone

at Rainworth Lodge, where his house resembled a museum, containing cases of stuffed birds and other natural life exhibits. Whitaker was
also a keen sportsman, botanist, fisherman and collector of curios. He
wrote a book on medieval dovecotes in Nottinghamshire, although
not all the examples were medieval and not all were even in the
county. He also had his own deer park and collected deer horns.

Whitaker had a penchant for writing poems, of which this is a mercifully brief example:

I know the south, I know the north,
I've seen the counties up and down,
Sailed in a yacht all round the coast
From Jura's Isle to Lerwick town.
I've seen cathedrals east and west,
And sung for joy of what I've seen
But the one spot I love the best
Is Rainworth, when the trees are green.

The original Bird Stone that Whitaker put up in Thieves Wood was
vandalised in the 1980s, and the replacement was erected to remind
passers-by of the event. At the same time it keeps alive the memory of
one of Nottinghamshire's eccentric characters who furthered our
knowledge of birds, dovecotes and other topics.

Mansfield Museum and Art Gallery holds the Whitaker Collection
of exhibits in its archive – they include the stuffed Egyptian nightjar
and are available for viewing by appointment.

90. Thoroton

Pigeon pie

Grid Reference: 763423

Directions: The dovecote is easy to spot when passing through the village.

Like the other free-standing dovecotes at Sibthorpe and Barton in
Fabis, the structure at Thoroton is one of the oldest in the county.
Dating from the Middle Ages, it is a circular, stone building with a
thatched roof. It has been much restored from the parlous state it was
in at the beginning of the 20th century. Joseph Whitaker (see Thieves

Wood) recorded that it is 17 metres round, 5 metres high and 1 metre thick. Dovecotes were solely in manorial, monastic or clerical possession until a law in the middle of the 18th century made it possible for people to build them on their own land. Most surviving dovecotes in Nottinghamshire were built after this act.

The dovecote

Pigeons were then kept for meat and generally eaten in the winter
months when other meat was scarce. After the initial construction of
the dovecote, pigeons came *almost* free, finding their own food in the
surrounding fields. Their dung was also valuable for manure, tanning
leather and for making gunpowder.

The protruding courses of brick around the building are a rat-
ledge, designed to deter rodents from climbing to the top to gain access to the birds. What is missing today is the glover on top of the roof.
This contained a number of holes for the pigeons to climb in and out,
with alighting ledges to facilitate this movement. Inside were hundreds of boxes for the birds to nest in. Whitaker noted that there were
more nesting places than the dovecote at Scarrington, and that they
were closer together.

By the end of the 19th century almost no more dovecotes were being built, although pigeon-keeping is, of course, still practised for rac-
ing purposes.

91. Upton

The crime of poverty

Grid Reference: 712543

Directions: Thurgarton Workhouse is north of the A612 halfway between
Southwell and Upton.

Built in 1824, Thurgarton Incorporated Workhouse is one of the
oldest examples of its kind in the country. It was the flagship of
the ideas of the Revd J.T. Becher (see Newark), who wrote *The Anti-
Pauper System* in 1828. This argued in favour of the transformation of
the Poor Law, and was to have a profound effect on the workhouse
system. The Poor Law Amendment Act of 1834 restricted paupers
from obtaining outdoor relief, which meant that for many the only re-
course from abject poverty was to enter a workhouse. These institu-
tions were run by a board of governors and combined the local
parishes, a number of which Thurgarton brought together.

The workhouse was deliberately designed as a deterrent: men

were separated from women – even their wives – and these two groups were further divided into the perceived deserving and undeserving poor. They were forced to do unpaid work, the men picking oakum, breaking stones and crushing bones while the women did the household chores. The regime was punishing. Work lasted 10 hours a day with Sunday free for prayer, and the food was mainly bread and skimmed milk, with a few vegetables and a little boiled meat three times a week. Large sections of the outside community lived in the fear that one day this might be their fate.

The loathsome Poor Law Amendment Act was finally repealed in 1929, Thurgarton becoming the Southwell County Institution. Unlike many similar workhouses, it has not undergone many structural alterations since it was built. The National Trust bought it in 1997 with a view to opening it to the public – Thurgarton Workhouse serves as a grim reminder of a horrendous system.

Thurgarton Workhouse

92. Watnall
The Holy Well

Grid Reference: 499456

Directions: The Holy Well is about 8 miles north-west of Nottingham. After the bakery in Watnall Road, turn second left and then right into Trough Road. The well is on the wooded side of the road on the brow of the hill.

The story behind the Holy Well at Watnall is that one day in the 19th century a priest once blessed a small sick boy there, bringing about his miraculous recovery from an incurable illness.

All the spring water around here came from the same source and until problems arose with the water in the 1980s, the landowners, Hardys and Hansons, had used it in the brewing of all their beer. The brewery has used mains water since and the land has been sold for housing.

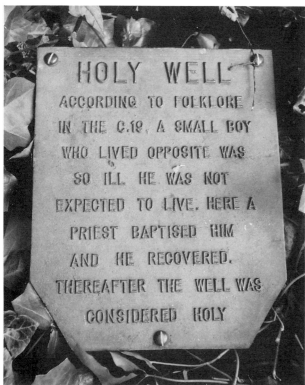

HOLY WELL
ACCORDING TO FOLKLORE
IN THE C.19, A SMALL BOY
WHO LIVED OPPOSITE WAS
SO ILL HE WAS NOT
EXPECTED TO LIVE. HERE A
PRIEST BAPTISED HIM
AND HE RECOVERED.
THEREAFTER THE WELL WAS
CONSIDERED HOLY

The entrance to the well

93. Welbeck

The duke's tunnel vision

Grid Reference: 568754

Directions: South Lodge is east of the Mansfield-Worksop road and 3 miles south of Worksop. Turn into Broad Lane opposite the signpost to Whitwell. The lodge is at the end of the lane.

Welbeck Abbey is a part of the Dukeries along with Clumber, Thoresby and Rufford, although Rufford was never owned by a duke. The most famous duke to live at Welbeck was the fifth Duke of Portland, a man of staggering eccentricity. South Lodge is one of the forty such buildings made of Steetley stone and in the Tudor style that he erected over a 19-year period. The toilet and kitchen of many of these lodges were underground, meaning that steam could frequently be seen coming out of the ground. Behind this lodge is one of the exits of the tunnel system created by the duke. It is more than 1 mile long and begins at the side of the riding school stables.

Much of the legend which attaches itself to the fifth duke comes

South Lodge

from the sixth duke's step-sister, Lady Ottoline Morrell, but it is sometimes difficult to ascertain which are the stories that have been embroidered on. She described him as a "lonely, self-isolated man". Owner of the estate on the sudden death of his brother, Lord Titchfield, the fifth duke was then only 21. In his early years he seemed quite normal, and for a few years was MP for Kings Lynn. It was after this period that the bizarre behaviour started.

At Welbeck Abbey the duke lived in only four or five rooms and had two letter boxes – one for mail coming in and one going out. He did not mix with his peers but got on well with his army of workers, whom he told not to greet him but to treat him as if he were a tree. They set off to their tasks with a donkey and an umbrella and were largely employed in digging underground tunnels – the duke's obsession. He built great expanses of them, the longest stretching 1.5 miles to the old Worksop road. The tunnels were not small in width, either, being capable of holding two carriages at a time. He built stables almost grand enough to rival the Spanish School in Vienna. Excavation was by traction engine and steam plough, and all rooms and tunnels were lit by thousands of gas jets and heated by hot air.

All this time the duke maintained his anonymity, riding everywhere with the curtains of his carriage drawn. Some said that his grandiose follies were conceived to give employment to as many people as possible. Others held that reluctance to spoil the look of the house occasioned his going underground. This is perhaps a little too rational, and the truth could be that it was a symbol of the duke withdrawing from the normal world. In spite of his reclusion, the duke often showed awareness of the outside world. He gave £4000 to Turkish hospitals during the Russo-Turkish war and sent an entire ship full of food and beer to the British in the Crimea.

The duke continued building rooms underground. There was a suite of library rooms, afterwards turned into supper rooms, although these were so near the surface that fanlights issued in the daylight. The ballroom – an extraordinary piece of work, especially for such a loner, one might think – was the biggest in Europe without supporting pillars. The duke spent millions of pounds on his crazy projects, and on his death in 1879 building work ceased immediately. He died at Harcourt House, the home of his brother, Lord George Bentinck.

When the Welbeck estate passed to the sixth duke he had at first to step across planks where the floors should have been. His first reaction was to leave the place as it was, although he gradually managed to restore normality.

94. West Bridgford
The old Trent Bridge

Grid Reference: 582382

Directions: West Bridgford is 2 miles south of Nottingham. Immediately south-west of Trent Bridge is a small traffic island where the remains of the bridge are located.

The old Trent Bridge* represents a long history. The River Trent was once a vitally important political and geographical boundary, essentially dividing the north of the country from the south. The significance of a bridge linking north and south near Nottingham was enormous.

Before the existence of the first Trent Bridge, passengers would

The remains of the old Trent Bridge

---

* It was never called Nottingham Bridge because it is only relatively very recently that the city of Nottingham was enlarged to the river.

have ferried themselves across the water. Then in 924 Edward the Elder, Alfred the Great's son, built the first bridge. It was no doubt made of wood with stone piers, and he defended it with a fortress at the southern end. This was the most important bridge since the time of the Romans.

The bridge was replaced about 1156 by Henry II's Heth Beth Bridge, which contained a chapel dedicated to Saint Mary. It has been compared with the bridge chapel at Bradford-on-Avon. Chapels such as these were common in the Middle Ages as at the time the upkeep of roads and bridges was seen as a religious duty. The chapel had two chaplains and marriages were solemnised there.

In 1364 the bridge was in such a poor condition that an almost entire rebuilding was necessary. In spite of Edward VI granting a considerable sum of money in 1551 to the upkeep of the bridge, it was ruinous in 1635. It was damaged further in the Civil War, repaired with 15 arches, and repaired again in 1725.

The royal arms displayed on the present bridge relate to 1840, when Queen Victoria and the Prince Consort took a journey to Belvoir Castle via the old bridge. The bridge was becoming totally inadequate and in 1870 a new one was built, the width of which was doubled in 1926.

The remains of the old bridge, much ignored by passers-by, date from the old Heth Bridge of 1364.

95. West Stockwith

Going against the flow

Grid Reference: 785946 (West Stockwith basin)

Directions: West Stockwith basin is opposite the Waterfront pub at the south entrance to the village.

West Stockwith is one of the most northerly of the Nottingham-shire villages and sprawls along the bank of the River Trent facing East Stockwith in Lincolnshire. From the Humber estuary upstream to Cromwell, seven miles from Newark, West Stockwith is

The floodbank and the River Trent

one of the places where the phenomenon known as the *aegir** – pronounced to rhyme with "vaguer" and often spelt "eagre" – occurs.

The aegir is a tidal wave caused by a rise in the sea tide at the estuary. It surges up the Trent, reversing the normal water flow, and can reach a height of over 2 metres. Gainsborough is 27 miles upstream and huge barges there have been tossed about. Smaller vessels have been vigorously rocked as far as 47 miles from the river's source. The spectacle can occur at any time of the year, but it is at its strongest when both the estuarial tides are at their roughest and the flow of the river is lowest – in March and September. Unsuspecting river passengers have often been taken by surprise by the aegir, although seasoned travellers have exploited it to reduce their power consumption.

Flood control at Cromwell is the reason for the absence of the aegir any farther south, and over the years the tidal bore in general has become a little tamer owing to dredging.

---

* The aegir is witnessed in other rivers, although dictionary definitions more particularly restrict it to the Severn and Humber estuaries alone.

96. Winkburn

Last signs of Basford

Grid Reference: 710585

Directions: Winkburn is 8 miles north-west of Newark. At the T-junction in the village, the Burnell Arms is on the west corner of Winkburn Lane.

Tiny Winkburn belonged to the Knights Hospitallers of the Order of St John of Jerusalem around the middle of the 12th century. After the suppression of the monasteries, Henry VIII gave Winkburn to Thomas Burnell and the Burnells were lords of the manor for over 200 years. The former Burnell Arms was named after them.

For most of the second half of the 19th century the pub was run by John Rickett. It is now a private house and bears the faint remains of a Bradley's Ales advertisement on the south-facing wall. This was perhaps the most distant tied house in the T Losco Bradley estate.

The Midland Brewery is first mentioned in 1874. It was in Northgate, New Basford, between Palm Street and Rye Street and Anthony Poynton was the director. He was followed by Malden & Dell in 1888. It was not until 1907 that Thomas Losco Bradley bought the business from the bankrupt Malden & Dell and started a successful concern. It was one of the last Nottinghamshire breweries to survive into the second half of the 20th century.

The Bradley's sign on the former Burnell Arms

As well as this tied house, Bradley had about 40 others including: Sir John Borlase Warren (Canning Circus), King William IV (Sneinton), The Adjutant White (St Ann's), The Porter's Rest (Cromford Street), The Barley Corn (Raleigh Street), The Elm Tree (Hoveringham), The Ram (Beauvale), and The Prince of Wales and Rutland Cottage (both at Ilkeston).

"Bradley's Brilliant Ales" disappeared when Shipstones Brewery bought them out in 1954, and the brewery premises also went with redevelopment. There is another painted advertisement for Bradley's Ales in Maples Street, Hyson Green.

97. Wollaton Park

A remarkable conservatory

Grid Reference: 532391

Directions: The Camellia House is south of Wollaton Hall. Opposite the entrance to the Industrial Museum is an iron gate. Walk through it and up the path to the building.

It is easy to miss the Camellia House while visiting Wollaton Hall and the Industrial Museum, although it is worth a visit to Wollaton for this alone. Built in 1823 with a facade entirely of glass and cast iron, it may well be the first building of its kind, coming about a year before the similar one at Grange Park in Hampshire. The parts came from metallic hothouse manufacturers Clark and Jones of Lionel Street, Birmingham. Standing next to the terrace, this was the sixth Lord Middleton's attempt at a winter garden. The Camellia House itself cost £10 000 and included heating equipment which also provided a hot water supply to the hall. The exotic camellias added an astounding £1400 to the bill. The identity of the builder is uncertain, although Jeffrey Wyatt (later Wyatville) would probably be the best guess: he built Lenton Lodge, the village lodges and servants' hall and had previously built similar structures to the Camellia House.

The gardens were considerably more extensive than today, and were thought by many to be second only to those at Chatsworth House. There is a car parking charge for entrance to Wollaton Park grounds.

The Camellia House (see previous page)

98. Worksop
The pub out of town

Grid Reference: 565792

Directions: Manor Lodge is signposted approximately 1 mile west of the centre of Worksop.

Robert Smythson built Hardwick Hall, Wollaton Hall and Long-leat. It is also probable that he built Worksop Manor and Manor Lodge, the former of which was destroyed by fire in 1761. The lodge was built for Roger Portington, the keeper of the seventh Earl of Shrewbury's park. Remarkable for its kind, this huge building once had an additional fourth floor and a flat roof rather than the present pitched one. It is now a pub.

Worksop Manor Lodge (see facing page)

99. Worksop
The station for the gentry

Grid Reference: 585797

Directions: The station is within a few minutes' walk of the centre. Take the Carlton road (B6045) and it is on the left after Clarence Road.

The impressive station at Worksop, formerly owned by the Manchester, Sheffield and Lincolnshire Company (MSL), has amazingly survived demolition where others have long since disappeared. Designed by Weightman and Hadfield of Sheffield in the Jacobean style, and built by James Drabble of Carlton-in-Lindrick in white Steetley stone, it was opened on 17 July 1849. It was built in such style to encourage use by the aristocracy from the mansions of the Dukeries. As the nearest station to Worksop was at Eckington in Derbyshire, Worksop station proved very popular in the beginning. It made it easier for people to travel, and was a welcome source of export for such local industries as malt and Windsor chairs.

Worksop Station

In 1875 the Midland Railway Company negotiated use of the line by building a route from Mansfield to the east of Shireoaks. Neither of the lines showed great public support, however, and there were now many complaints by businessmen about the slowness of the trains and the shabbiness of Worksop station. An attempt was made to make it more presentable for the visit of the Prince of Wales in 1881. Crowds of people lined the streets to see him on his way to visit the sixth Duke of Portland.

The MSL became the Great Central Railway in 1897, and with this change of name came a change of image and a greatly improved station. What had formerly been dubbed "Muchly Slow and Late" and "Money Sunk and Lost" was now extended, with a canopy and waiting and refreshment rooms added to elongated platforms. It was a success, and Nottinghamshire is fortunate that the results survive until today.

100. Worksop

The semi-detached time machine

Grid Reference: 591802

Directions: Mr Straw's House is about five minutes' walk from the train station. From Carlton Road take the right turn into Blyth Road and Blyth Grove is the second on the right.

Blyth Grove in Worksop stands on the outskirts of the town. The setting little prepares the unwary for what lies within number seven – an amazing time capsule greets the visitor on the threshold. The house has hardly changed at all since the 1930s when time stood still for its occupiers.

William Straw senior was a grocer and seed merchant with a shop in Bridge Street in the centre of town. He married Florence, the daughter of David Winks, and the couple lived above the business premises. William's great thrift must have had a tremendous influence on his two sons, William Straw junior and Walter, and the technological advances of the 20th century virtually passed the whole family by.

The slightly younger Walter was less academically inclined than his brother and he started working full-time in his father's shop when he left school; William junior went on to take an MA at London University and then teach in the City. When the family moved house in 1923, most of the furniture went with them. The house had been built about 1905 and William Straw senior paid to have it redecorated throughout. It was never considered necessary to redecorate again.

William Straw senior died in 1932 and Walter started to run the shop. Florence followed her husband to the grave in 1939, and William quickly returned from London. The remarkable thing, though, is that the house was preserved by the brothers as it was when the parents were living, becoming almost a shrine to Florence and William senior. Their father's coats still hung in the hall, the calendar of the year of his death was unmoved and his pipes were hung by the fire on a rack. Their mother's bedroom curtains remained drawn after 1939.

Walter enrolled at the Arthur Murray School of Dancing and had girlfriends, but William, certainly the more dominant brother, did not allow a woman into the house after the death of their mother. There was obviously friction between the brothers, although not externally. In later life Walter allowed himself the luxury of a van, but William did not permit him to leave it at Blyth Grove.

Walter died in 1976 and his brother died in hospital 14 years later. William, always a keen local historian, bequeathed about £1.5 million to the National Trust. The house stayed as if preserved in aspic. 7 Blyth Grove contained thousands of objects – furniture, ornaments and food products from the shop – of a past era. The modern age was not allowed a look-in. Many objects had William's notes explaining their uses attached to them, the purpose of this being as much an *aide-mémoire* for the ageing William as a self-conscious desire to record things for posterity.

Mr Straw's House

Realising the importance of the house, the National Trust bought it and kept it as it always has been. Admittance can now be booked by the public. The house next door, number 5, is a kind of interpretation centre for number 7. Mr Straw's House can only be visited by prior appointment. There is a museum car park opposite. On arrival you pay at the interpretation centre. Opening hours are from 13.00 to 16.30, Tuesday to Sunday from the beginning of April to the end of October.

Sources

Listed below are just some of the many sources consulted in the research for this book:

Board, Joan, *The Old North Road through Babworth Parish*, J.H. Hall & Sons Ltd (1992)

Bradbury, D.J., *Secrets of Sherwood*, Wheel Publications (1987)

Brand, Ken, *The Park Estate, Nottingham*, Nottingham Civic Society

Brand, Ken, *Watson Fothergill Architect*, Nottingham Civic Society

Brewer, E. Cobham, *Dictionary of Phrase and Fable*, Galley Press (1981)

Edwinstowe Historical Society, *Edwinstowe Past and Present*, Newark and Sherwood District Council (1987)

Evening Post (various)

Foster, Val, *Clumber Park*, National Trust (1995)

Guilford, Everard L., *Nottinghamshire*, Methuen (1910)

Lyth, Philip, *The Pinfolds of Nottinghamshire*, Nottinghamshire County Council Planning and Economic Development, Heritage Team (1992)

Magnusson, Magnus (Ed), *Chambers Biographical Dictionary*, Chambers (1990)

Marchand, Leslie A., *Byron. A Portrait*, Pimlico (1993)

Mee, Arthur, *Nottinghamshire*, King's England Press (1938)

Megill, Brendan, *The Parish of Kingston-upon-Soar 1538-1988* (date and publisher unknown)

Nottingham Guardian (various)

Nottingham Journal (various)

Nottinghamshire Federation of Women's Institutes, *Nottinghamshire Village Book*, Countryside Books (1989)

Pevsner, Nikolaus, *The Buildings of England. Nottinghamshire*, Penguin 1951

Pevsner, Nikolaus, *The Buildings of England (revised edition). Nottinghamshire*, Penguin (1979)

Scoffham, Ernie, *A Vision of the City*, Nottinghamshire County Council Leisure Services (1992)

Severn, John, *Dovecotes of Nottinghamshire*, Cromwell Press (1996)

Shaw, Tony, *Windmills of Nottinghamshire*, Nottinghamshire County Council Planning and Economic Development, Heritage Team (1995)

Summers, Norman, *A Prospect of Southwell (revised edition)*, Kelham House (1988)

Trade directories (various)

Waltham, Tony, *Sandstone Caves of Nottingham*, East Midlands Geological Society (1996)

Warner, Tim (various articles in *The Newark Advertiser*)

Weir, Chris, *The Nottinghamshire Heritage*, Phillimore (1991)